Read what students, parents, educators and business professionals have to say about Power Reading:

My speed has more than doubled, my comprehension has increased and my test scores have improved.   S. Trio, Student

I doubled my speed and improved my comprehension. I especially gained from the ways of handling books, magazines and journals. I recommend this course to others.   R. Herr, Dentist

Power Reading has improved my reading and study comprehension. Tests are much easier. I recommend this course to anyone.   G. Beasley, Student

I really enjoyed the Power Reading course. It has improved my comprehension and speed immensely. I now have these skills under my belt and can use my time more efficiently. It has helped me with my classes and grades. Thanks again!
D. Kawasawa, Student

We are so proud of the progress of our son's improvement since he took the Power Reading course. Kenny has improved in all of his classes at school since he took the course. Thanks for all the help and thanks for the confidence you have given Kenny.
Mr. and Mrs. P. Terry, Parents

I can read faster with excellent comprehension and I recommend this course to everyone.   D. Wein, Commercial Pilot

Amazing! I think this course is amazing because I have increased so much in my speed. I can read a book almost twice as fast and I have more comprehension now.   M. Carson, Student

It has improved my reading skills — both speed and comprehension — and has provided me with information on more efficient reading methods. The course is very satisfying.
J. Padilla, Bank Executive

The best book I've ever read on speedreading!

I've always wanted to read faster, much faster. Some years ago, I began reading books about speedreading, also called "rapid reading." These books helped me, and I could see a progress in my speed, but usually I quickly fell back into the old patterns and went back to a slower reading speed.

What immediately hit me when I began reading Rick Ostrov's book, **Power Reading**, is his emphasis on making learning speedreading a natural process. Just like me, Rick doesn't like the speedreading methods that try to force you into doing something that feels terribly odd and uncomfortable to you. Speedreading ought to be something enjoyable, he says. When you read his book, you really feel that you have a very experienced and patient teacher helping you to take each step forward.

In almost all the other books I've read about speedreading, you just get served some techniques that you're told to practice, but usually it isn't explained why. And when you're doing those exercises, you're often feeling uncomfortable and unnatural doing so. Not so with **Power Reading**. When I followed Rick Ostrov's methods, it all seemed both enjoyable and natural. I really liked the whole learning process. And all the time I felt that I really knew what I was doing. Rick uses only methods and techniques that are really helpful. "If you don't really understand what you're reading, you're not reading at all," Rick says, "no matter how fast you 'read'."

What further characterizes **Power Reading** is that it's very realistic. The author doesn't promise you that you'll be able to read thousands of words per minute like most other authors do. Instead, he promises you that you'll be able to double your reading speed, or even triple it. It is possible for some people to read thousands of words per minute, but that's not normal for most people. But doubling or tripling one's reading speed is a very satisfying accomplishment. Just imagine what it would mean to be able to cut your daily reading time in half! And I like Rick's realistic promise much better than the hyped and unrealistic promises. (next page)

(continued)

After having used Rick's methods systematically for some time, my reading speed has generally about doubled. Sometimes I read even faster. But my normal reading speed now lies somewhere between 400 and 800 words per minute.

*Rick Ostrov has written a very useful and impressive book, **Power Reading**. Even if you've given up on learning how to speedread, you should strongly consider giving this book a chance.*

It's really, really good, and I strongly recommend that you invest in this book if you want to read more in less time and enjoy the whole process.

K. Dahl, Internet Product Developer
Power Reading Graduate - 2001

*****Power Reading** is well organized, easy to read. Having been in the educational business for quite some time, it amazes me how little emphasis educators put on a basic skill such as reading. I enthusiastically recommend **Power Reading** to any teacher or student.*
Dr. Joachim Vogeler, Professor, Louisiana State University

I think this course should be taught in schools. It makes school work a lot easier and helps improve grades.
A. Moreno, Student

My reading speed has increased and my comprehension has improved. I would recommend this course to everyone.
M. Wilson, Mechanical Engineer

*I think **Power Reading** is a very good course. It has helped me improve my reading abilities tremendously. I have to admit that I was skeptical of the course at first. I didn't believe anyone could read that fast. But after doing the course myself, I find it is very efficient for doing homework. Your course has cut in half the time it takes me to do my homework, and it makes it a lot easier to find answers in my textbooks. I thank you very much for helping me help myself.* S. Curt, Student

POWER READING

The best, fastest, easiest, most effective course on speedreading and comprehension ever developed!

Rick Ostrov

The Education Press
www.speedreadingcourse.com

2002
Third Edition

Published by
The Education Press
P.O. Box 195
North San Juan, CA 95960
www.educationpress.com

Ostrov, Rick
POWER READING : The best, fastest, easiest, most effective course on speedreading and comprehension ever developed!
1. Education. 2. Speedreading 3. Comprehension
4. Speed Reading. 5. Study. I. Title

ISBN 0–9601706–1–8

Printed in U.S.A.
10 9 8 7 6 5 4 3 2 1

Third Edition

This new 2002 Third Edition of Power Reading is dedicated to everyone who believes that the ability to learn gives us the power to create a better future for ourselves, our families and the whole world.

Preface

I am happy to have the opportunity to write the preface to this new and latest edition of *Power Reading*. Over the years that this course and book have been successful in helping people read faster and more effectively, there have been many changes in the world. This makes the benefits that you will achieve from *Power Reading* more important and more valuable than ever.

The need to read, cover, understand and use large amounts of information grows with each passing day. The tools of the information age, such as computers and the Internet, have placed huge amounts of data within our reach. At the same time, these tools have increased the burden on us to cover more just to begin to acquire any area of knowledge. To become an expert and to keep up with the latest developments in any field almost requires the advanced *Power Reading* skills.

The first page of this book explains my background. I have always loved to read and learn. In college, I specialized in information and communication among people or within any system whether it was biological, physical or electronic — this is the field known as cybernetics. I witnessed the beginning of the information explosion in the 1960s. This information explosion has progressed at an ever accelerating pace and will continue to do so in the future.

As a result, *Power Reading* becomes more important every day.

Power Reading is different from all of the reading programs that came before it. Over the years since it came out, I have seen other programs try to borrow some of the techniques and terms and even the title of this course, but I believe that you will find that nothing else really compares with *Power Reading*.

Power Reading is purposely simple and easy to learn. It emphasizes comprehension first and then teaches you how to speed up your reading. It teaches you with your own reading materials while you work or study. It shows you what to do step-by-step to become one of the most powerful readers in the world.

Power Reading is so effective because it has evolved from years of successfully teaching thousands of others how to do something that I love to do myself — read and learn!

I welcome you to *Power Reading* and look forward to helping you now and in the future.

Table Of Contents

Preface   ix

Table Of Contents   xi

Course Instructions   xiii

1st WEEK — LESSON I

Chapter 1   How Well Do You Read Now? Initial Exam   1
Chapter 2   How Much Can You Expect to Improve?   13
Chapter 3   What is Power Reading?   21
Chapter 4   Looking at the Whole — The Preview   27
Chapter 5   Your Approach   33
Chapter 6   Varying Speed — The Regulator   37
Chapter 7   Comprehension and Concentration   45
Chapter 8   Another Regulating Method   51
Chapter 9   A Look at the Whole   55
Chapter 10   1st Week's Exercises   61

2nd WEEK — LESSON II

Chapter 11   Increasing Your Speed   67
Chapter 12   Perception   73
Chapter 13   Why You Read the Way You Do   81
Chapter 14   Changing Your Habits   89
Chapter 15   Reading Various Types of Materials   95
Chapter 16   Newspapers, Magazines and   101
             Correspondence
Chapter 17   Pleasure Reading   109
Chapter 18   Reading and Drilling   111
Chapter 19   2nd Week's Exercises   115

3rd WEEK — LESSON III

Chapter 20   Mid–Course Exam   117
Chapter 21   Technical Reading   123
Chapter 22   Study   127

Chapter 23   Note-Taking   143
Chapter 24   Vocabulary   147
Chapter 25   How to Research An Area   153
Chapter 26   An Advanced Preview Technique   157
Chapter 27   3rd Week's Exercises   159

4th WEEK — LESSON IV

Chapter 28   Fundamentals Again   163
Chapter 29   Reading and Thought   165
Chapter 30   How Do You Know What's True?   171
Chapter 31   Speedy Speedreading — High–Speed Techniques 175
Chapter 32   High–Speed Drills   189
Chapter 33   4th Week's Exercises   193

30th DAY

Chapter 34   30th Day — Final Exam   195
Chapter 35 Conclusion: Power is Knowledge Plus   201
             Common Sense

BIBLIOGRAPHY   205

INDEX   211

POWER READING:
Course Instructions

In the past 20 years alone, more discoveries have been made and more information has been published than in all of mankind's history up to this point. How can the average person keep up with this explosion of information? What is to happen to students, parents and everyone else who need to stay ahead of this changing world?

These are the people for whom this book is written.

Power Reading is actually a course in book format. It is a distillation of years of teaching and research. It contains the techniques I have evolved through teaching myself and thousands of other people how to become more powerful, more effective readers.

I love to read; I always have. I became interested in reading faster soon after learning to read. I was my own first research subject and I continued experimenting later in high school and college with friends who were willing to cooperate.

After completing college, I continued my studies in this area. I spent years professionally teaching reading improvement, speedreading and advanced technical reading and study skills. The courses and seminars I taught always had guaranteed results, and the cost to the students enrolled was usually hundreds of dollars.

During this time, I studied, researched or experimented with almost every method known in the field. This included years of teaching with the largest commercial speedreading program, the Evelyn Wood Reading Dynamics Course. In fact, a film was made of one class I taught. The class consisted of engineering professors on the faculty at the University of Texas. This film has been shown on television for years in almost every major city in the United States and many foreign countries. It has also been used in advertisements, lectures and seminars.

Over the years, I have personally found that everyone can learn to read better and faster, but only a few individuals achieve miraculous results. The range varies, but almost all of my students have learned to read at least half again faster, and most doubled their speed without difficulty. At the same time, they equaled or increased their comprehension and enjoyment. This includes individuals from all walks of life: students, executives, housewives, professionals, blue-collar workers, doctors, secretaries, lawyers and many, many others.

These are not the usual spectacular results claimed in TV commercials and newspaper advertisements, but they are honest, realistic and achievable by everyone with a minimum of effort. Advertising, of course, sells the sizzle and not the steak. It is true that you "can" read two to ten times faster, but it is far more likely to be two than ten.

How to Do This Course

We will start with realistic expectations, and, with a reasonable amount of effort, we will achieve them. *This won't happen magically or overnight; it will be a gradual, building process over the next four weeks. It takes at least this long to effectively change any old habit and begin to firmly establish a new one.*

This course is divided into four lessons. *It is a four-week program and you should do one lesson each week.* Each lesson is subdivided into chapters for easy study and later reference. Once each week, you should pick a definite time to do each lesson just as though you were attending a class. During this period you should cover all the material as presented in the lesson. Then, during the week, you can refer back to individual chapters for further study.

One week later, at the same time, on the same day, you should cover the next lesson, and so on. If you wish, you may preview or read ahead, but, if you do, you should still sit down and cover the entire lesson again at your assigned time. This course continuity will ensure your maximum gain.

You can do this course as a group with your family or friends. If so, don't lose anyone along the way, and be sure that everyone understands each step and does each exercise.

How This Book is Different

This book differs from other books on reading improvement and speedreading in several respects. Most books on reading tell you generally what you should do, cover many theories, give helpful advice and tell you to push yourself. Many of these are filled with reading passages and multiple choice tests that may or may not be interesting, meaningful or beneficial to you.

This course is specific in its recommendations and directions, and you will choose your own reading materials. Use materials from school or business or use pleasure material. You decide.

You do not need to attend lengthy classes; all you need to do is use the techniques as taught in this book on everything you read for the next 30 days and practice at least 150 minutes during the four weeks. This comes to 5 minutes of practice a day for the 30 days, plus at least 10 minutes of normal daily reading.

In one month, you should be reading about twice as fast as you presently do in most materials. Some people will be reading faster than this and some will be reading slower, but the average person will be going about twice as fast.

During this course we'll cover many basic areas in a simple, straightforward survey approach. You will learn not only how, but why you do each step in changing your reading styles. Later you will be asked to use the bibliography and read other books and articles about this subject. I want to encourage you to come to your own conclusions and opinions in this as well as every other field.

By the end of this 30-day program, you will find it easier to sit down to read and research an area. You will learn how to cover a large amount of material and cull it until you have isolated the essentials and pinpointed the crux of the issues.

You'll be able to read easily in many types of material and will be comfortable with varying your speed to obtain the comprehension and enjoyment you desire. No longer will you be limited to just a single reading rate as most readers are; the basic rate at which you read everything will increase and your comprehension should improve.

This gives you an idea of what you can expect from this course and what we will cover. Later we will discuss more specific goals and expectations for you, but now, let's begin and find out how well you read presently.

- Note -

If you need a new prescription for glasses or have a medical condition that causes you discomfort or pain when reading, you should consult your optometrist or doctor before beginning this course.

1st WEEK – LESSON I

The beginning of wisdom is the definition of terms.

Socrates

Chapter 1

How Well Do You Read Now?

Initial Exam

How well do you read now? Most people, when asked this question, respond: "Oh, I read pretty well..." or "Well, I enjoy what I read..." or "I don't read too fast, but that's because I am very careful and don't miss anything."

Most people feel that they read well, but they don't know precisely what that means. As with most things, some objective standard is necessary for measurement. Without some measure you would not know how much you actually had improved upon finishing this course. You would probably end up feeling that you improved somewhat, but you wouldn't know for sure just how much. Some measure is needed to show how well you read now and how much you progress through the course.

How well you read is based on two factors: the first is speed and the second is comprehension. If you read extremely fast, but can't understand the material, then you might as well not have read it. For all practical purposes — and as we will later define reading — you haven't. At the other extreme, if you read too slowly, you may never have time to finish what you start. You may not be able to keep up with what you need to read and know. Both factors are important.

1

Speed

Reading speed is usually measured in words per minute (wpm). Your wpm is actually the average number of words you read in one minute of a reading test that lasts several minutes. But it is not the only way to get an idea of how fast you read. For example, you might read a book in a few hours, days or even weeks.

If you take weeks to finish a book, you shouldn't feel bad. There are many people who have never completed reading a single book in their entire lives. And, incredibly, a few of them are college graduates. Only 15 percent of the people in the United States check out and read 80 percent of all the library books. About half of the people in this country have not read a book in the last four or five years. So even if you take weeks to finish a book, you are far ahead of many people.

If it takes you a week to read a book, we could say your reading speed is a book a week, or 1/7 of a book a day, or so many pages an hour. The same could be done with newspapers or magazines. As long as we use the same measure and time period, we could see if you were improving by comparing the amount you read now and the amount when you finish this program. For some people, this might be a more meaningful standard, but the measure commonly used and accepted is words per minute (wpm).

Unfortunately, most reading tests are too short. This stems from limitations on time and testing facilities, and when millions of tests are being administered, these limitations become critical. The average reading test covers a short passage and takes little time to read. Unfortunately, this does not correspond to the bulk of daily reading that most of us do.

That is why our reading test period will be 10 minutes long. This will give you enough time to settle down and relax. A shorter time span sets up an artificial test situation and promotes a tendency to speed up. Everyone likes to do well on tests and naturally tries hard to push himself or herself, but that is not the purpose of this test. Its purpose is to get as accurate a measure as possible of how fast you read when you are relaxed and reading normally. I have found this measure to be the most useful one for the average person.

Comprehension

In our 10-minute test, you will choose your own material to read. This will help give you the most accurate evaluation. You can also repeat this test in several types of material if you want.

People generally tend to read better and more accurately in material they find interesting. One thing we want to establish is how well you read in your normal daily reading. Then later, for comparison, we'll repeat this test midway and at the end of the course in the same material.

Speed is relatively easy to measure, but comprehension is another matter because it varies with the individual and material as to quality and amount. As yet, there is no single "ruler" to measure the scope, view and depth of the human mind.

You already have your own methods, approaches and habits of reading, and they are strongly cemented by years of experience.

They are more entrenched than many other habits because you use them so often. Everyone feels comfortable reading in his own manner and usually thinks he is understanding what he reads. Of course, background, experience and interest all affect your ability, results and appreciation.

You know how much you have understood from what you read, but is this all there was in the material? Whom should you ask? Who should decide what you should get from the passage? How important is it that you remembered or guessed more correct answers on a particular test than someone else?

Did you understand more when reading than you could remember later when taking the test? Does this mean you didn't comprehend it when you read it or that you couldn't remember it later? It is difficult for any test to account for these factors when it is used to "measure" comprehension.

Standardized tests often favor students who come from similar cultural, economic and intellectual backgrounds as those who created the test. A streetwise orphan may not score as high on a standardized test as a private school student, and yet, she may be much more intelligent. For these and other reasons, there is a good deal of controversy going on about the efficacy of standardized tests, but no final conclusions have been reached. Standardized tests are not bad, but they do have their limitations. As long as these limitations are kept in mind, such tests can be useful. At present, they are the only practical way to look quickly at and compare the millions of people in schools, jobs and other institutions.

There are many standardized reading tests available. Many of the leading ones are listed in the bibliography and are available through your school or library. You can take one now and another at the end of this course if you wish, but it isn't necessary.

One alternative to the standardized test is the essay test in which the student writes down or summarizes his understanding of the material. Then it must be checked for correctness. The main criticism of the essay test is that of subjective evaluation. Whoever grades the essay may vary the standards from one essay to another.

However, we will use this type of test for several reasons. There is no limit to the type of test material that can be used, and you can cover as much material as necessary. Also, you can correct it yourself for quality as well as quantity of response. This requires a little honesty, but if you have enough desire to take this course, you certainly have enough to grade your own test honestly.

Essay tests also have their difficulties in that many

people have had little recent practice summarizing in written form. On the other hand, most people talk about current events, sports, fashions or other topics in a summarizing form. In addition, most people write summaries when they write letters. For all these reasons, we will use an essay test to check your comprehension.

You will summarize what you have read after the 10-minute reading period. This way, you will find out how fast you read. Then you will check and see for yourself how accurately you understood and remembered what you read. This is the most important reason why we will use this form of test.

Test Material Selection

This brings us to the type of material with which you should test yourself. It should be a non-technical book, something you would normally read and enjoy. Choose something you can continue later in the course. Remember, you will need more pages later for your mid-course and final tests, at least twice as many for each. So pick something you can read a part of today, and then pick up in two weeks and again at the end of the course. At each point, you will read a new section for 10 minutes for a comparison and to measure your progress. It is necessary to use the same material on the three tests to ensure an accurate comparison, so be sure to pick something long enough.

I suggest you pick a simple fiction or non-fiction book. Difficult, technical or study material is a special category of reading and is something we will cover in Lesson III in the third week. If you wish, you may choose something technical for a supplementary test, but you should not use it for your primary measure. Use something fairly simple and average for you.

Now, stop at this point and select your test material.

Select Test Material

Preferably a fiction or non-fiction book. Be sure you will have enough material for the mid-course and final evaluations.

Now that you have your test material, you need only a few more items and we are ready to begin.

You can use various methods to time yourself. A clock, wristwatch, kitchen timer, stopwatch or alarm clock will suffice, or you can have someone else time you. Or, you can use the supplemental Power Reading CD described on the last page of this book. Also, you will need a pencil or sticky note to mark your ending spot and a dictionary.

I cannot emphasize enough that you must relax and read as you normally do in order to get an accurate evaluation. You are not in a race or being compared with anyone else, but you are trying to find out just how well you actually do read now. So be honest. Otherwise, you will just be fooling yourself.

Do you have all your materials? Are you ready? Good! Remember, read as you normally do and, at the end of 10 minutes, stop and mark your ending point.

All right, ready, begin reading.

Read Test Book for 10 Minutes

PLEASE
Do not continue this course until you have completed the initial 10-minute reading.

Very good. Did you mark your ending point? If not, do so now.

Now summarize as fully as possible what you've just read in the last 10 minutes. Do this on the Initial Reading Summary on the next page.

Initial Reading Summary

Date:_____

Book Title:_____

Page began reading:_____

Page ended reading:_____

Summary:_____

_____

_____

_____

_____

_____

_____

_____

Now, read your summary over and add anything you wish. Take your time and be as complete as you can.

Calculate Your Reading Speed

At this point, we're going to do a little arithmetic. Many people feel this is the hardest part of the course, but just follow each step and we'll get through it.

Your reading speed is expressed in how many words you read in one "average" minute. This is called "words per minute" (wpm). To determine this, we need to find the total number of words you read in the 10 minutes. We will then divide this total by 10 to get your reading speed, your "wpm".

Look at the Example, then Fill In Your Answer.

Step 1: First we'll count the number of lines of print on a full page of the material you read. We'll count every line as a full line.

Example 1: __30__ lines of print per page.

Now write your actual count in the blank below.

Answer 1: _____lines of print per page.

Step 2: OK, now let's count the number of words on 10 typical lines. Count even small words as full words. I also recommend that you count punctuation marks as words, for as words are similar to building bricks, so punctuation marks are the directions for how and where to lay them.

Example 2: ___80___words on 10 typical lines.

Count and put your actual figure in the blank below.

Answer 2: _____words on 10 typical lines.

Step 3: To get the average number of words on a single line of print, we have to divide your Answer 2 by 10.

Example 3: $\dfrac{80}{10}$ = 8 words per line

Now do your calculation.

Answer 3: $\dfrac{\text{(Answer 2)}}{10}$ = _____ words per line.

Step 4:   So far, so good. Now we can get the average number of words on each page. Just multiply Answer 1 by Answer 3. Look at the example first:

Example 4: __30_ lines per page
          x 8 _words per line
          240 words per page.

Now you do it, using your Answer 1 and Answer 3.

Answer 4: _____ (Answer 1)
          x _____ (Answer 3)
          _____ words per page.

Step 5:   Now we need the number of pages you read. Count the pages and round off to the nearest half page.

Example 5: ____11_____ pages read in 10 minutes.

Answer 5: _____ pages read in 10 minutes.

Step 6:   Now we can find the total number of words you read in the 10 minutes. Just multiply Answer 4 by Answer 5. See the example:

Example 6:   240 words per page
          x 11 pages read in 10 minutes
          2,640 total number of words read in 10 minutes.

9

Now calculate yours:

Answer 6: _____ (Answer 4)

     x _____ (Answer 5)

    _____ total number of words read in 10 minutes.

<u>Step 7</u>: Almost there; only one more step. Divide Answer 6 by the number 10 (for the 10 minutes you read). This gives you your speed in words per minute (wpm).

Example 7: $\dfrac{2,640}{10}$ = 264 wpm

And now yours:

Answer 7: $\dfrac{\text{(Answer 6)}}{10}$ = _____ your speed in wpm.

This is how fast you currently read.

    Now that we know your reading speed, let's take a look at your comprehension.

    Look over your initial summary once again and then answer the following questions:

1. Did you feel you understood what the author said?
Yes_____No_____

2. Do you feel you got the main ideas?
Yes_____No_____

3. Do you feel you got the basic facts?
Yes_____No_____

Of course, you could answer yes to all three of these questions and still not have understood the author. So to check yourself and find out how accurately you did read your test material, I'm going to have you quickly read it over again. This time, as you reread it, look to see if you really did understand it correctly and completely. Afterwards, you'll check your summary and answer more questions about the material. So now reread the test material.

Quickly Reread the Test Material to Check Your Comprehension

Now look at your summary again and then answer the following questions:

A. Did you understand it as well as you thought earlier?
Yes_____No_____

B. Did you understand the main idea or ideas correctly?
Yes_____No_____

C. Did you get the basic facts?
Yes_____No_____

D. Did you get enough from your first reading to satisfy you as you look back now?
Yes_____No_____

E. How much do you feel you correctly understood?
All_____Most_____Enough_____ Not Enough_____
Little_____

F. Do you feel you understood it when you read it, but couldn't remember as much when you went to summarize it?
Yes_____No_____

G. Are you satisfied with your present level of comprehension?
Yes_____No_____

H. Would you like to improve your comprehension?
Yes_____No_____

I. Do you feel you need to work most on comprehension, speed or both?
Comprehension _____Speed_____Both_____

Now you know how fast you read and should have a good idea of how well you can understand what you are reading. Of course, both your speed and comprehension will vary from one type of material to another. As we have seen from our discussion of tests, there are limitations no matter what form is used, because trying to measure the view and understanding of the human mind is not as simple as measuring the length of a board or the speed of a car. If you wish, have one or two other people read your test passage and essay. This can give you a good crosscheck.

If you are like the "average" reader in the United States, you would be reading about 250 words per minute and scoring 70% on a standardized test. You would fall within the range of 225 to 275 wpm and 65 to 75% comprehension. This gives you an idea of how you compare with the "average" reader. It is not too important, but most people are interested in their "standing."

What is important is how much you want to read and how much you get from what you do read. Can you read everything you want? Can you understand it? How much can you expect to improve?

Now, if you have been just reading along and haven't actually taken the test yet, then stop here and do so now. Go no further until you do. Otherwise, you won't know your true beginning rate, because as you read on, you will learn how to read faster.

Chapter 2

How Much Can You Expect to Improve?

How much you can improve your reading skills depends entirely upon you. How much do you wish to improve? What reasons do you have for improvement? How hard will you strive to achieve your goals? How consistently will you apply yourself toward achieving these goals?

Some people feel that reading improvement is only for students or professionals. Yet many of these "average" people have the same problems. They cannot keep up with the reading they need and desire to do. Often they would like to be able to read newspapers, magazines and correspondence as well as do some recreational reading. Many people wish they could pursue hobbies or continue their educations, but don't because they haven't the time to do the necessary reading and study. Others, unsure of their ability to do so successfully, do not make the attempt.

Almost everyone wants to know and understand the world around him or her more fully, but many lack time to read the daily news, much less pursue further studies. However, there is a solution. They can learn to read with power.

Anyone who can read can learn Power Reading. It is simply putting more systematic, conscious control and energy in your reading. As you will learn in this course, it is not hard. There is no age or educational limit. Some may need to start and work within a limited vocabulary range at first, but this stage is soon surpassed. Yet, many people still feel they do not need to learn to read any faster because it isn't necessary for them; they do not need the skill. Do they?

This is a question each person must answer for himself, but there are some obvious needs for information.

Most housewives wish they knew more about how to

make the best purchases and the wisest use of their money. How can they stretch their dollars? What products do the best jobs, last the longest, are the most effective and actually save the most money? Are they always the cheapest? How can a family get good, nutritional food at the lowest prices? And why are prices so high and going up? Or are they? Who sets prices and how is it done?

Who sets the budget in your household and decides how much is spent on what items? Who does the taxes? How are your investment, savings and spending decisions made? Are they made in the best manner? What accounting or managerial principles could be applied to make them more effective for you? What are the best and wisest answers for your family's financial future?

How safe are the products you want to buy? Do you know if the advice you are receiving from your lawyer, doctor or accountant is up-to-date and correct? How can you know? Why are the decisions being made in government the way they are? What are the prospects and outlooks for the future? What changes are affecting the world and how do they affect you?

Can only the rich afford the answers to these questions? No, absolutely not! Answers and information applicable to these and countless other questions can be found in books and periodicals and on the Internet. They are waiting there for you to consult and use. Locating and reading is all they require.

Almost everyone recognizes that the success of any decision is based on the accuracy and completeness of the data on which the decision is to be made. If your data is incomplete, then your understanding of the situation will be inadequate, and the success of any consequent decision will also suffer.

In every field, a prerequisite for success is preparation. Without seeking out, collecting, organizing, analyzing and digesting information for use, there would be little progress in any area. Science is largely based on the successful utilization of this process. Our modern civilization flows from its application. All businesses, organizations and individuals must do this in order to make correct decisions and succeed.

The most successful people in every field need to keep abreast of the latest information in order to stay on top of new developments and opportunities. This information comes in written form and reading is your key to its access. Today, more than ever before, knowledge is power. Knowing what to do and when to do it is based on information. How much you have is largely up to you.

As the world's pace of change accelerates, it is increasingly necessary to know more just to survive as well as to succeed. Democracy and a free society are dependent on an informed electorate. Not only does information have to be available, but people need to be able to read and understand it.

Television and radio can keep you abreast of current events, but too often it is only at a superficial level. Thirty to forty-five seconds of exposure can only tell you that a problem exists. To get a fuller, in-depth understanding of any area or issue requires reading. The necessary information is in written form. It is available when you want it and are interested in it. Anytime you want information, you can find and obtain it at your library, bookstore or on the Internet. This is true whether it concerns a monumental government decision or what is the best type of appliance for you to buy.

You may think as we go on that I am a salesman for your local library. I am, but that is not my primary purpose here. I have another.

Success and Survival

The mind works by taking in information and making decisions based on this data. Your individual success and survival is dependent on the decisions you make. Our survival as a free, democratic society is dependent on us all. For better or worse, we will survive together or go down together. In a modern, technological world full of nuclear, chemical and biological weapons and facing global environmental issues, this is an inescapable reality; and the choice is ours.

Fortunately, unlike existence in a totalitarian society, the quality and quantity of information you assimilate is largely up to you. The greatest experts in every field are waiting to advise you on any questions you may have. You need only the ability to consult them. No king, emperor or ruler who ever lived had the quality of advice and information that is available to you today.

The key is being able to read and understand it quickly and accurately. Without this skill, all the advice will go unheard and unheeded. It might as well not exist.

The quality of your data determines the quality of your decisions. The quality of your decisions determines the quality of your life. And the quality of your life affects us all. So how much do you wish to improve your reading abilities? The decision is up to you.

Earlier I gave you a realistic appraisal of what your improvement might be. Can you expect miracles? Can you read thousands and thousands of words in a minute? Can you flip through a book and have it memorized? Can you go to sleep with a book under your pillow and wake the next morning to find that you know it all without effort? Can you read 7 or 10 or 20 times faster without effort and with total comprehension? Are you looking for the magic pill to take or the big secret that will miraculously make you a super-reader?

Determination

We all know that most worthwhile achievements take time, determination and work. This course is no different. Reading is one of your most basic mental skills and it won't change overnight. But it can be changed. It won't be too hard, but you will have to work at it. What will determine the amount of permanent gain you make and how much you will improve? It is your determination, your persistence and the amount of use you make of what you will learn in this course that will determine your success.

Results

Your lifetime increase in reading skills will be proportionate to the degree that you apply yourself to understanding, studying and using the information as laid out in this program.

If you quickly read over and do little or nothing with this material, then your gain will be minimal. If you put in a 10 percent effort, it will result in about a 10 percent increase. If you "dabble" at it, but do the drills occasionally, you should obtain a comfortable 50 percent gain without too much difficulty.

If you follow the instructions exactly, filling out your daily log and using the reading techniques as given in this course, then you can anticipate approximately a 100 percent gain in your reading speed and efficiency. This is a doubling of your reading power. This means you can have access to an entire extra lifetime of information!

As you read the books and articles in the bibliography, you will find this is consistent with better programs. To become a "speedy" speedreader and read 10 or 20 times faster is unrealistic for the average reader. Studies show most people who attain such speeds in courses quickly fall back to their old rates once the course is over. Often they are not really reading or understanding what they are seeing.

Such courses will quickly push you to go over and practice far faster than you can read. The underlying theory is that when you slow down, it will be at a rate much faster than when you began. This is the "push up" method. When used primarily, it produces temporary high speeds as you go over many words, but often leaves a great deal to be desired in the area of comprehension. Tests given to students of such courses have shown an actual decrease in comprehension although their speed is much higher.

Usually such courses will push you to speeds far in excess of those at which you can read, then try to stabilize your speed at these high levels. Following this is an attempt to bring back comprehension at these new high-speed levels. It doesn't work effectively enough as you will find out by talking to their graduates and reading the bibliographical references. Most graduates later lose their speed because of a lack of practice. But how could this be when they read every day of their lives? The reason is their course emphasized speed at the sacrifice of comprehension, and the students had to revert to old habits in order to read with understanding.

This is why Power Reading has you increase your speed in a gradual manner, and the emphasis is on using the techniques as you read rather than quickly trying to push up your speed. I have found that most people are not interested in "speedy" speedreading, because at high speeds your comprehension and retention of detail are reduced. This was shown by one test of "speedy" speedreaders in which they got only 50 percent comprehension, less than when they started. Such comprehension is inadequate and impractical for most everyday reading needs.

Practical Increases

I have found that most people desire practical increases in their reading skills. These are:

- Better Comprehension.

- Faster Speed.

- An improved ability to read, understand and remember technical or study material.

- An ability to quickly read or skim over a great deal of material and to pick out what is important and deserves a more careful reading.

These are the four areas covered and skills taught in the four lessons of this course.

This is what you can expect, and now is the time for you to think about how much you want to accomplish.

Choose your goals now and write them down. Remember, you can learn to read 10 percent faster, 50 percent faster, 100 percent faster or more. It is your choice, but it must be something that you realistically want and will work to achieve.

My power reading goals are:

1. Comprehension _____

2. Speed _____

3. Other _____

4. I will work _____ minutes/hours daily for the next 30 days to achieve these goals.

It Actually Works!

Surprise! It actually works! With this book, you can advance at your own pace... but, you must suspend all disbelief and actually __do__ the exercises. I used to be the world's slowest reader — now I breeze through tech manuals and newspaper articles and, before you know it, I have so much time to do other stuff.

Mr. Soolsa, New York
Power Reading Graduate — 2001

If you have completed testing yourself and picked your goals, then let's continue and see just what Power Reading actually is.

Chapter 3

What is Power Reading?

Does Power Reading consist of being able to read books as fast as you can turn the pages? Is it a method of avoiding the effort that goes into study or work? Do you still read everything at a single speed, only faster? The answer to all of these questions is the same: "No."

Power Reading is more than just reading faster, although that is one of its basic tools. *Power Reading is a complete approach to, and handling of, written prose information.* It concerns how and what you read as well as how fast you read. Your overall ability to cover, assimilate and use information is far more important than the simple increasing of the speed at which you read the words on a single page.

Power Reading is of no use if you cannot comprehend effectively and remember the information later. It should help you to increase your abilities in these skills as well as reading faster. In some cases, you will become more selective in what you read. In others, you may actually spend as much total time reading, but achieve a far greater understanding than you would have in the past.

The purpose of Power Reading is to increase your overall ability and efficiency in handling written information. This doesn't always mean simply reading faster. Surprising as it may seem, I have taught many of my students to slow down and read more carefully at first, because they were not really understanding what they were reading. Then, once their comprehension became more effective, we began to work on increasing speed.

This comprehension problem is more common than you might suspect. Studies have shown that as many as one third of the people in this country cannot understand much of what they should be able to read; they are functional illiterates. This does not mean they cannot read at all, but that they cannot read, comprehend and use much of the information necessary for their effective survival in this day and age. Our civilization uses the written word for communication, instructions, forms and directions; these vital, written means of communication are beyond the ready understanding of many poorer readers. To a large extent, this leaves them outside the mainstream of life.

There is no need for these people to be so handicapped, because in the vast majority of cases, they can overcome their deficiencies. It does take work and persistence, but it can be done. Most people do not fall into this category of the functionally illiterate, but there are increasing pressures on almost everyone to push, hurry, cover more and be more effective. The flow of daily events has grown in both speed and volume until it has overwhelmed many people, because the skills and methods they were taught to handle information are no longer sufficient. These older methods evolved and were developed to cope with a slower pace of life and a slower pace of change.

Today, everyone needs to read and know more. Twice as many books are being published today compared to just a few years ago, and the number of professional journals has increased many times over. Students are pushed to read 4 to 10 times more in college than a generation ago. The increase of experimentation, knowledge and development in every field has led to a flood of information that can drown the unprepared. More than 1,000 books a day are published worldwide. There is so much more to learn and keep up with today than ever before in man's history.

Part of the response to this avalanche of information has been to give up and stop reading. Another has been a tendency to merely skim over everything. This is as bad as reading everything slowly and never finishing anything, and in some cases, it can be worse. Both are outcomes of the same approach; that is, to read everything at the same rate and in the same manner.

If you have the habit of being limited to a single rate, as most readers do, and learn nothing more from this course than to read different materials at different speeds depending on what you need and want from the material, you will have made significant gains. You will become one of the most effective readers in the world.

Power Reading is more than just reading faster. It encompasses a broad variety of skills geared to allow you to become as efficient as possible in your taking in and handling of written information. Naturally, you may find a good deal of carryover into other areas of your life as the principles for effective handling of written information also apply to other types of information you take in and use.

Because of your past, you are set in your reading habits. Reading is something we do every day of our lives, and our established reading habits are among the strongest we have. This also makes them among the most difficult to change. Yet, because we do use them so much, the rewards of changing them are equally great.

At the same time, most readers have firm opinions about reading. It is a natural tendency to hold strong opinions about anything you have experience with, and reading is no exception. But, a warning: these opinions can pose a barrier to establishing new habits, and they can be used by a student to justify and reinforce old ones. Naturally, I don't want you to do this, and neither do you.

In some ways, teaching Power Reading is like teaching tennis or golf to someone who has played for years and already has established habits. For such a person, learning new habits can be difficult. It is easier for a teacher to start from scratch with a youngster who is an aspiring Tiger Woods. This is true for both the instructor and the student. It is not impossible to reverse bad habits, but it does hinge on your determination and persistence. Change does not always come easily, but it does come if it is pursued diligently.

To change your habits, you must be determined not only to try the techniques and ideas given here, but to use them continually in your daily reading. It will not be enough just to read about them in this book. And while it is important, it is not enough just to read faster; there are other skills to learn, such as your strategy and method for approaching the material to be read.

Power Reading begins with systematic methods for handling written information. Three of the most basic are: 1) Looking at the Whole, or previewing; 2) Your Approach; and 3) Varying Speed.

The first, "Looking at the Whole," consists of getting the overall picture. You are finding out what the material is all about and getting ready to read it. This is a previewing step before you read the material. You are looking ahead before you get there.

"Your Approach" will be determined by the information gained from the preview step. It is how you read. Some materials you will breeze right through, while some will take more time. Others you'll want to read several times or study carefully. But, you need the information from the preview to make this decision intelligently.

The third method, "Varying Speed," comes into play while you are actually reading. Not only will you want to vary your reading speed from one type of material to another, but as you read anything, you will want to speed up in some parts and slow down in others. Sometimes it may take you as long to read one page with 10 ideas on it as it takes you to read 10 pages of a novel covering a single idea, such as a description of scenery. This is fine. It's the way you should read, varying your speed to get what you need and want from the material.

These are some of the basic tools of efficient readers. You already may use one or more of them as you read, and if so, excellent. You can sharpen up the ones you have and be that much farther ahead in using them all. If you are an average or below average reader, you may find them new to you or seldom used. If this is the situation, then your gain will be even greater when you acquire them as new habits. In either case, let's look at each of them in more detail. They are the tools which, when used correctly, will allow you to put some real power in your reading.

Chapter 4

Looking at the Whole — The Preview

The first step in more effective handling of written information is to look quickly at the whole picture to get an overview of what you are about to read before you actually read it. This is "Looking at the Whole," or previewing.

This preview prepares your mind to take in the information and to think about the particular topic. This is similar to looking over a mountain before you begin to hike up its side. This way you can choose the best path available. It is like looking over the whole forest before you begin to walk through it. It is like looking at a map before you get on the highway or start out on your trip. This way you have an idea of where you are, how far you have come, how far you have to go, and what lies ahead. Understanding the whole idea and flow of the material helps you to piece together and correctly understand each part as you come to it. Naturally, a piece of a jigsaw puzzle makes more sense when you have already seen the whole picture.

It is amazing how few people do this when they read. Most people, out of habit, begin to read everything from the first word, whether it is a book, article or whatever, without looking ahead or knowing anything about it. In some cases, it is a conditioned response from school days. Whatever was assigned, they read from beginning to end with little thought except to complete the assignment. This habit slipped into the rest of their reading and thus limits their ability. Wherever they happen to start reading, they doggedly plug ahead from that point, word by word.

A similar situation exists with the spoken word, but usually there is little choice. When someone talks to you, each word comes in succession, one after the other. Usually, you have little control over the situation. You cannot speed up or slow down the speaker's pace. Many times, you do not know where the person is heading and, too often, he may not know himself. You are dependent on listening to the flow as it comes, word by word. It is usually around 120 words per minute. President John F. Kennedy was an extremely fast talker and spoke about 300 wpm. In addition, he was a naturally fast reader. But fast or slow, speech still comes out word by word.

Reading is the same habit process for most people. They start at the beginning with the first word and plug along to the end. Many times, they are not quite sure just what the material said, although they are quite sure that they saw and read each word as they went through it. Such readers seldom look ahead. Often they pay little attention to the title page of a book and completely ignore the table of contents or index. It is ironic that many of these readers "know" better, but still ignore these steps. It is simply a matter of habit. Commonly, such readers find themselves gazing at pages they have seen without having an idea of what messages the pages convey. What is worse, they often will continue on without understanding what they are reading.

Faster speed isn't a complete solution for this problem. You can lose yourself while reading quickly as well as reading slowly. Concentration is what counts, and keeping your mind concentrating on the material begins before you start reading. You can "warm up" your concentration.

Athletes warm up before they begin a contest. This loosens up their muscles and helps prepare their bodies for the activity. A preview serves a similar purpose for your mind. It prepares you for what you are about to read. It helps shift your attention from whatever daily affairs preoccupy it and helps focus it on the information to be read and absorbed. It also makes it easier for you to read and comprehend, because it gives you an idea of what you are going to cover. Then you can read as a friend, not as a stranger, to the material. You see the whole idea before you read each part; you know where you are, where you are going and what you are looking for.

An example of "Looking at the Whole" is when you read the headline of a story in the newspaper before you actually read the story. You are getting an idea of what it concerns. Then, when you read the story, you are looking for more information to explain it further. The material isn't strange or unfamiliar to you if you are working from a base of information and adding to it.

You wouldn't pick up a magazine from a newsstand and buy it without looking over its contents. Normally, you look over several magazines and pick out the one that interests you most. While doing this, you look over the whole magazine and get an idea of what it is about and what it contains before investing your money in it. In this way, you ensure a wiser investment and use of your money. The same should be true for your time.

"Looking at the Whole" is your first step in effective reading. It consists of quickly looking something over, usually from beginning to end, before you read it. You are looking at the whole selection and finding out what it covers. You actively question as you do this step. Try it with the remainder of Chapter 4, then return to this point.

First Question – Q1

What is the main idea? Is this material fiction or non-fiction? Do you want to remember it? If it's fiction, what category does it come under: adventure, novel, mystery, romance? When does it take place? Where? What is it about? Who is the author? What else has he or she written? Have you read any of these other works? Is it a non-fiction work? What is the subject matter: current events, politics, economics, history, ecology, armaments, war or business? What is the author's main idea or contention? Do you want to read it and, if so, how thoroughly do you want to read it?

Some of the time you can easily find the answer to these questions. Often you will have a definite idea in your mind of what interests you and what you would like to read. Then the choice is easy. At other times, the answers may not be so obvious or you may not be sure exactly what you want. There will be times when you look for something specific or have a definite need. At such times, the question to answer is whether this particular selection fills your need.

Second Question – Q2

Then comes the second question, or step, in "Looking at the Whole." Once you know what the main idea is, you should ask yourself: "What do I want from this material?" Why did you choose it? What is your purpose? What do you hope to get, accomplish or achieve from reading this particular item, book, article, piece, paper, magazine or whatever? If the answer is nothing, you may not want to read it. Strange as it may seem, this realization alone can save many people a great deal of time.

Too many people feel compelled to finish reading something just because they started it. Not knowing what it is about, they start it and then feel uneasy about putting it down unfinished. And, even if they do put it down, they feel guilty afterwards. There is no reason to be enslaved by such an attitude. You should decide how to invest your time in the best manner for yourself and not be directed by an absolute rule from some past teacher. If you do not wish to read something, that is fine, put it down.

Third Question – Q3

When you know what you want from the material, there is a third step or question to ask yourself: "What do I need from the material?" Is there something here that you need to know for your job, school, hobby, etc? Do you need the main conclusions, facts, opinions, projections, arguments, lines of thought, author's name or references? Do you need to remember the information? For how long? Will you be using it in the future? In what capacity? What is going to be required of you that is contained in this information? You may need nothing from the material and this too is important.

Asking and answering all three of these questions are the essential parts of "Looking at the Whole," of focusing your attention sharply, of preparing yourself to actually read the material. While you look the material over quickly, you are trying to answer these questions. They are the purpose of previewing, and they will help prepare your mind to read the material. At the same time, answering them serves to focus your attention on what you are doing and why you are doing it. It will aid your concentration and allow you to look for new information when you go back to read the material. Previewing is one of the keys to active, effective reading. "Looking at the Whole," or previewing, is the first step to Power Reading.

The Three Questions – The 3 Q's

Once again, these three questions that you ask and answer for yourself while "Looking at the Whole" are:

Q1 What is this material about?
Q2 What do I want from the material?
Q3 What do I need from the material?

When you have answered these questions, then you will be ready to read the material in the most effective manner possible. You will know where you are going.

To get some practice at "Looking at the Whole," do the following drill this week.

Pick five books and five magazines at random. Take any one of the books and look it over quickly, asking yourself the three questions listed above and answering them. Then do this with another book. Now do it with a third, but this time take no more than one minute. Do the same on the fourth and the fifth taking no more than a minute for each. If you now feel confident that you can "Look at the Whole" and answer the questions easily and comfortably in no more than a minute or two with any book, then continue on. If not, practice some more. Take another five books and repeat this drill until you are confident of your ability to preview any book and answer the questions in a minute.

Now take one of the magazines and pick an article or story from it. Look it over quickly and answer the three questions. Do the same with another article. Now take another magazine and repeat the procedure. Do this until you can easily pick up a magazine, find out what it is about and do the same with any article in it.

You can read the first or last sentences in paragraphs as these introduce and summarize the main ideas presented. You can read introductory and concluding sections, look at the index, pictures and graphs, as well as the title page, table of contents, introduction, and so forth. Remember, the idea is to quickly "look at the whole,"and not to stop and concentrate on one part at first.

These drills may seem frivolous until you realize that you need to work with these procedures, step by step. Then they will become part of your daily reading habits. After practicing this process slowly, and then naturally speeding up, it will take you little time or effort when you read. Each time, as you preview something before you read it, you will be beginning to take conscious control over your reading habits.

Improving the conscious control of your mind is one of the most important aspects of becoming a more effective reader. Doing these drills will help and will make you more conscious of taking control of your daily reading habits. Your old habits are unconscious ones. Deeply ingrained, they can be displaced only with conscious effort and application of new reading habits.

With practice, these new previewing habits will soon become part of your daily reading patterns and will give you the information to choose your best approach to reading the material.

Chapter 5

Your Approach

"Your Approach" refers to how you read the material. It can vary from a simple, straightforward reading to an intensive, careful study of the material. You can float along and "live" a story or carefully examine each point of a presentation. Which approach you choose will depend on your answers to the three questions answered from "Looking at the Whole" and several other factors. How much time can you afford for this material? How important is it to you? What is your previous experience with this type of material? Are you going to be responsible for the information? To what degree and how soon? All of these are important factors in choosing your approach to reading the material.

If you are reading fiction for your own pleasure, you might start at the beginning and continue reading until you complete the selection. Here there are no constraints. Some sources on reading improvement tell you never to do this. They say, "Time is money," and no matter what you are reading, you should look ahead and thoroughly preview each selection, each chapter or each page. This is a correct approach for non-fiction, technical or study material, but not for all materials. For example, when reading for your own enjoyment, you should read as you please. Naturally, you wouldn't want to know how a mystery novel ended before you finished it. So, your approach will vary with your purpose and the selection.

One of the basic purposes of this course is to give you a variety of reading tools and to put you consciously in charge of choosing and using them. I do not want to give you a single, unchangeable set of rules to memorize and follow. In the first place, it wouldn't work. One single approach is not universally applicable. Second, as individuals become better readers, they usually become more independent and capable of making up their own minds. This is what I want to encourage you to do as much as possible. Third, in the final analysis, you know best what you want to read, what kind of a reader you want to be, and what you need. You will need to use and try the methods given here, but you will also need to use your desire and common sense to change your habits.

One of the worst habits many readers have is "wasting" or "filling" their time with reading. Usually, this doesn't promote efficient reading because the purpose is simply to pass the time, to entertain yourself momentarily. If this is most of your reading, it can affect you when you try to read differently. You too may have developed this habit without even realizing it. This isn't reading to understand, enjoy or use the information; it is reading simply to fill up your time, to occupy yourself while time passes, or to put off other things until you finish reading "this one story." Naturally, in this case, the process of reading can easily lengthen until it takes up all the available time.

Some people do this with a lot more than reading. Instead of thinking about what they actually want to accomplish and then doing it, they let whatever activity they're doing drift along until all their time is gone. They may never finish what they set out to accomplish.

I'm not saying this is bad or that you shouldn't do it, but it is apparent that this runs counter to the process of actively, consciously taking control of your reading habits. The difficulty here is that this can become the basis of a person's reading habits. When this type of reader needs to read faster, he finds it's difficult, if not impossible, at first.

Awareness of this tendency can help a great deal in overcoming it. Consciously deciding what you want to read and why will handle most of the rest. It can be done.

Notice that I'm not saying you shouldn't enjoy what you're reading or that you should rush through it. I am saying ask yourself what are you doing and why are you doing it. This is the key to taking control of yourself, which is what you are trying to do with your reading. You want to be able to read rapidly as well as slowly, to be able to enjoy reading; what you don't want is to be stuck with a single reading approach.

Your approach to the material should be made consciously. Many times you will be reading for general information and will be getting everything you want and need from a single reading following a quick preview. Other categories such as technical, difficult non-fiction or study materials may take one or more rereadings before you can fully grasp, remember and use the pertinent information.

Remember, Power Reading is more efficient reading, not just reading faster. The entire process also includes understanding the material more fully and being able to remember it longer. Later, we shall see that this often requires a multiple reading approach, particularly in more difficult material. At other times, a single reading approach will suffice, and in between are numerous alternative approaches.

As we go along in this course, we shall cover in more detail specific approaches for specific types of material and purposes. You will learn to choose the best approach based on these various factors, and you will learn to vary your speed while you are reading.

Chapter 6

Varying Speed — The Regulator

Are you ready for a change of pace? Are you ready to start doing something different? Are you ready to start reading faster?

Well, here we go.

Beginning right now, I want you to put your index finger down here under this line of print. That's it. Now continue reading, but also move your finger along under each line as you read.

Using Your Finger as a "Regulator"

That's good, keep it up. If you are right handed, naturally you will use your right hand. Use the left index finger if you are left handed. Now don't try to read faster than normal or push yourself at this time. Just move your finger along, under each line as you read it. Oh yes, be sure to look at these words and read them, not your fingertip.

Doing this, you are beginning to take control over your

automatic reading habits. For awhile, you are going to use a "regulator" to regulate and control your reading speed. It also will help you change the eye focus patterns that cause you to read slowly.

Before you can have full control of this process, you must read with your finger just to get used to it being there. If you are having trouble understanding this with your finger down here, or if it gets in the way and feels uncomfortable, then turn this book upside down and simply run your finger along under each upside down line for a few minutes until you get used to the feel of it. Then turn the book right side up and continue reading. Once you are used to using your finger when you read, it will be much easier to control your speed.

Gradual Transition

Our immediate objective is to start the gradual transition from old habits to new ones. You are the one who already has decided to do this. You are the only one who can consciously carry it out. Already you have begun this process of taking conscious control by using your finger and moving it along under each line as you read.

See, it's not so hard to be a better, faster reader; you've started already. This may be what you tried to do as a child in grammar school. At that time, you were stopped because it was a crutch that could become permanent and hinder you. Now it's all right because we're using this technique in an entirely different manner. We're using it as a tool to allow you to consciously be aware of how fast you are reading. Soon we'll use it to allow you to speed up and slow down at will. You'll begin to consciously regulate your speed.

Right now you may even feel a little silly, but you needn't be embarrassed. I have had students who felt for awhile that they would have to quit the course because they were too embarrassed to read this way in front of their friends. They were afraid of being teased. I told them to tell their friends it was their doctor's orders. No, not their psychiatrist, their optometrist. After the laughter, I asked which was more important, their lifelong increase in reading ability or their temporary embarrassment. They decided they could handle their friends' teasing and stayed in the course. Naturally, they were so happy with their results, they were more than glad they stayed in the class. Any embarrassed feeling you may have will pass as you become used to using a regulator and increase your effectiveness. Then, with the tables turned, you can tease your friends about how they read.

Some new paperbacks you may have to open and "break in" gently by turning and smoothing down the pages so they'll stay flat easily. You may need to hold them open with one hand while you read with the other. Start with the cover and then work toward the middle of the book, 10 to 20 pages at a time.

"Breaking In" a book so it is easy to hold and turn the pages.

Now what I want you to do is to pick up something fairly easy to read and read it for 5 minutes. (Pick something other than your test material because you want to save that for later in the course.) Don't try to speed yourself up as you read, but read naturally, at a comfortable rate, using your finger for 5 minutes. Be sure to read for full comprehension.

Turning Pages and Using Your Finger as a Regulator

Pick and Read Your Own Easy Material for 5 Minutes

You may have noticed an increase in your speed already. Many people do, but not everyone, so don't feel bad if you didn't. If you did increase your speed at this point, it's a bonus.

You may have felt uncomfortable as you read, but this is to be expected. After all, you cannot easily change a lifetime's habits in 5 minutes. It will take some practice to become comfortable. By the way, you are still using your finger, aren't you? Good.

Already Changing

Remember, right now as you use your finger, you already are beginning to regulate your reading patterns. This simple technique will eventually help you break through your old habits. Then you will be able to regulate your reading rate at will. Every time you stop using a "regulator," you will be countering this process, slipping back and reinforcing your old habits, and you don't want that.

Comfort

There is no need to be concerned about your comfort. It will return. This changeover is like breaking in a new pair of shoes. The old pair is more comfortable at first, but the new pair will be able to get you a lot farther. And your comfort will return once the new pair of shoes is broken in. It won't take long, a few days to a few weeks. So have a little patience and don't give up, no matter what. You'll be happy with the results.

No Magic

I cannot stress strongly enough that the mere reading of this book to see what it says will only do you a little good. What will do you a lot of good is taking the techniques as I give them to you, trying them out, and then using them daily. A few minutes of trial is insufficient, but using them day in and day out will give them a chance to work for you. You must give yourself a real chance to work out of your old habits and into the new ones. There are no short cuts or magic formulas. This is the only way, and with determination, you will succeed.

In a little time, anywhere from a few days to a few weeks, your comfort will return as you "break in" these new habits. Then you'll not only be comfortable again, but faster and more efficient as well. This should be your goal; give yourself a month to achieve it.

Why Use a Regulator?

As you've been reading, you may have asked yourself: "What good will reading with my finger do me?" This is a good question.

As we are going to see in the next few chapters, the basic patterns of your perception and reading are automatic and below the level of your normal conscious control. But there are ways to change. What I have found is that if you give the mind a simple task it can do on a conscious level, it will perform the difficult, subconscious tasks necessary to carry it out. This process is automatic. The mind will cause the body to perform the complex perception-analysis functions necessary for reading in this new way. It will correct your old habits at the same time. All you need do is use your "regulator."

Some courses use special exercises, materials or machines to try to do this same job, but the results are no better and often not as good. For example, you could spend days or weeks doing eye span perception-expansion exercises designed to help you see more letters and words at a single glance. Often the comment from students doing such exercises is: "I can see a wider area now, but I can't understand what it says." This comes from focusing one's attention on trying to see more instead of comprehending what is seen. It is difficult to concentrate on both at once.

Actually, as we shall see, you already have the ability to see a wide field. You use it every time you look at the horizon instead of a single object on it. Because of your reading habits though, you tend to perceive words in set patterns with a narrow focus. This simple technique of regulating yourself will begin to help you break up the old patterns of perception, and as you begin to speed up, you naturally will develop new ones.

Once again, all you have to do at this time is continue to use your regulator as you read. Don't worry about your speed. Just use this technique and be sure you comprehend what you read.

Chapter 7

Comprehension and Concentration

Using your finger as a regulator will help improve other important areas besides speed. Two of these are your comprehension and concentration.

Here's how it works: as you read with your finger, you will notice any words that you do not understand. You should stop and look them up. Do this even if you think you probably know what the word means from the context of the sentence or paragraph. If there is a doubt in your mind, don't hesitate. Stop and look up the word's meaning in the dictionary.

Have you ever had this happen to you? You are reading along and suddenly realize you don't understand what you're reading? Your mind is wandering? You are getting sleepy? I have had many students tell me that it happens to them all the time. What should you do? You should not just continue reading on automatically, hoping that it will come to you. Stop reading when this happens and go back to find where you got lost or started thinking of something else.

Continuing along without comprehension isn't reading; it's just a waste of time. When you read, it is like going through a forest on a path laid out by the author. There are turns to make and other paths to cross. There is an almost infinite number of trees or thoughts that can divert your attention, but there is a set path for you to follow as well.

If you find yourself off the path and realize that you are wandering in the forest, return to it. Do not just continue going along through the woods. You may have missed the turn you were supposed to take, so you need to go back to the point where you were on the path and find out what happened. When you understand the missing information, then continue down the path.

Comprehension

If you find any confusing words, stop and look them up, or else you may end up "reading" something different than what the author wrote. This is a great cause of poor comprehension. It's not that you totally don't understand the author, but that what you think he is saying is different than what he is actually saying. This can happen because what you think a word means may be different than what the author thinks it means.

When you speak with someone, you can always check to make sure that each of you understands the other. This is a two-way flow of communication. When you read, this opportunity doesn't exist; there is a one-way flow of written symbols from the author to the reader.

The written symbols represent spoken words. The spoken words themselves represent other things in the real world. Since you learned to speak as a child, your vocabulary is partially based on what your parents and others around you thought words meant and how they should be used. These meanings may not be correct, complete or applicable even though you have used them your entire life. No one is "to blame" for this. They just passed them along. Luckily for us all, there is a collection of word rules and meanings we can check against — this is the dictionary.

Unfortunately, the dictionary is not used enough. What often happens is the reader guesses at the word and continues. Then, what the reader thought the author meant is not quite what the author actually intended. Again, this stems from the fact that what the reader thinks a particular word means is not the same meaning that the author used. It might be close, then again it might not, but the dictionary is the place to find out for sure.

Suppose for a minute we consider each word to be a brick. The author has a building in his mind which he takes apart brick-by-brick and passes one-by-one (via printed or written words) to the reader. The reader then reconstructs them in his own mind, brick-by-brick (or word-by-word). Thus, if the reader exactly and correctly rebuilds the structure, he will correctly perceive what the author had in his mind.

Correct Reading

However, if he misses a brick or puts in a rock or a ball of dirt instead, or just inserts the brick sideways, he'll be altering some of the structure. Therefore, he may not understand the author or be uncertain about what he's saying. He'll have a building, but it won't be the same one. It may not serve the purpose and it may even fall apart.

Incorrect Reading

Reading is like putting a puzzle together. If what you're reading doesn't make sense, you've got a piece missing or sideways. The solution is not to continue reading in hopes that you'll get it, but to stop and find out what's wrong. Locate the missing or incomplete piece. Consult the rule book, the dictionary, as often as necessary.

Students are told to use a dictionary, but rarely is this taught so that it becomes a constantly used reference tool. And it is the most important tool a reader has.

You are not reading if you are not understanding, no matter how fast you go. So, the sooner you begin to use the dictionary at a moment's hesitation, the easier reading will become. Then you'll find you need to use it less often. The more you read and look up words, the more you'll understand and the easier the whole process will become. Remember, while the context often will show you the approximate meaning, only a good dictionary will give you the precise definition. So use your dictionary and be certain of your words. This is a fundamental rule of all reading.

Another problem that plagues average readers is that they often read so slowly that they become lost in some part and lose sight of, or can't remember, the whole. This is like not being able to see the entire forest because you're amongst the trees. It will resolve itself easily and naturally as you begin to read faster and better and preview the material ahead of time. Slowness, then, will no longer be a barrier to comprehension.

Comprehension is not a difficult subject. Just remember this:

Reading Without Comprehension = Not Reading but Wasting Time

You must decide for yourself if you are comprehending enough.

While you may be able to take tests and write essays, the only important measure of your comprehension is how well you can use what you are reading in your daily life. Only you can be the judge of this. If you have any questions about what you're reading, then reread it. A rereading, or recheck, will give you certainty, and this process will build your confidence in your comprehension. Take all the tests you wish, but no matter what your scores, look to yourself to ensure your fullest understanding.

Concentration

Over the next few weeks you'll notice a change. It will be easier to concentrate on your reading and studying when you use a regulator and look up words. This, once again, comes from breaking up your old habit patterns.

Your habits of concentration also have their established patterns and crosscurrents. Years of reading and studying with other things on your mind, not quite understanding what you are reading, being interrupted, and other factors, all can act to interfere with your concentration. The concentration patterns formed from these experiences also can be improved by using a regulator.

Probably one of the hardest chores I've had over the years has been to isolate what to teach, to determine what was necessary and what was not. This simple technique of regulating your reading, used over time, will produce the maximum amount of gain with the minimum amount of effort. It is one of the most effective new habits you can cultivate.

Now remember, we're starting off working on comprehension first. I'm not asking you to make an effort to read faster yet, and I certainly do not want you to let your comprehension slip. OK? Good. Make sure you understand what you want and need from your reading and, once again, use your dictionary.

Comprehension Improvement Drill

If you wish to drill on comprehension, do a 10-minute reading, essay and recheck every day. After you reread the material, add to your essay in a different color pen or pencil. On the rereading, look for what you missed the first time, look for anything you may have misinterpreted and note everything you got correct. Put these observations at the end of your essay and watch how quickly your comprehension improves.

If you have any question about what to do if your comprehension or concentration slips or is not as good as you would like it to be, come back and reread this chapter and do the comprehension improvement drill given above. If you've got it, then let's go ahead and look at an alternative regulator.

Chapter 8

Another Regulating Method

Here's another method for using a regulator. I like it better and many others do so as well.

Using a Pen as Your Regulator #1

Using a Pen as Your Regulator #2

Using a Pen as Your Regulator #3

You may substitute a ballpoint pen or a pencil for your finger if you wish. For many people, this is more comfortable and convenient. I prefer to use a ballpoint pen or a mechanical pencil with the tip retracted. You don't want to mark up your book needlessly or carelessly; they're much too valuable.

Try using a pen or pencil and see if you like it better.

Let your wrist do the moving instead of your whole arm from the shoulder or elbow.

Pick up something else to read besides this book and read for 5 minutes using your pen or pencil as a regulator. Remember, don't mark up the material, because it can make later reading difficult for you or someone else.

Read for 5 Minutes Using Pen as a Regulator. Move From The Wrist.

Did you like this method of using your pen or pencil better? Was it more comfortable? Many people find it easier and more convenient, because you do not have to move your arm as much.

You should shift back and forth between using your finger and your pen or pencil. Eventually you will decide on the method that is better for you. Some people use both equally, but most find one method more natural and comfortable than the other.

Take your time to decide which is better for you, and then keep on using it.

Chapter 9

A Look at the Whole

Now let's practice some of what we've been talking about.

Quickly preview this material and then carefully read it. It will cover what we have discussed and introduce some new data.

A Look at the Whole

Power Reading is more than just reading faster. It covers the entire field of effectively approaching, absorbing and using written information. Increased reading speed is one of its most important aspects, but not the entire subject.

Freedom from the set patterns and habits that slow your reading is one of the main benefits of this course. Gaining conscious control over how you read is another. You will get these results by using the techniques given in this course in your daily reading over the next month.

Previewing, or "Looking at the Whole," is the first step. It allows you to see where you are and what you have to read. It also helps prepare your mind for the particular type of material. This improves your concentration. While previewing, you are answering three questions. These are:

- What is the main idea?
- What do you want from the material?
- What do you need from the material?

The answers to these questions will be used to choose your approach to the material.

Your Approach is how you read the material. It can range from a single reading to a concentrated study of the material. Your background, previous experience with the type of material, specialized vocabulary and other factors also influence your approach.

Varying your speed as you read is another important tool. The more complicated the material and the more concentrated the ideas, the more carefully you will need to read the material. It is as important, but often more difficult, to speed up when the material becomes easier as it is to slow down when necessary.

Using a regulator, whether it is your finger, pen or pencil, is of paramount importance. You should not worry about speed this week, but concentrate on comprehension. Make sure you understand what you are reading and you get what you need from the material.

If your comprehension falters, do not continue on, hoping that it will return. Go back to where you did understand the material and come forward again. Look up any word you are unsure of in the dictionary; don't just depend on the context or guessing.

The use of your regulator will help you change your old habit patterns and establish new ones. It will also help you to overcome some of the things that have caused you to read slowly.

Why Do You Read Slowly?

Why do people read slowly? The answer to that is simple: most people finished learning how to read by the fourth grade. They still read the same way because they were never taught more advanced methods. They never learned to read faster or more effectively than at that level. Oh yes, they became smoother and improved through practice, but still were stuck with the same basic habit patterns and techniques.

The average reader, without knowing it, "regresses," or goes back over the same material as much as 40 times or more on a single page. When you do this, you are endlessly repeating what you did as a child. Only now you do it without thinking; you are subconsciously checking over what you read after you have read it. When you were young, you weren't sure of the words, and so it was natural for you to double check. After years of reading, it's become an unconscious, unnecessary and automatic habit. To stop it takes more than wishing.

Regressing is not the same thing as consciously deciding to reread a section, sentence or paragraph. Rereading is okay as long as you do so consciously and deliberately. All effective readers do this. But previously, without realizing it, you've been "regressing" and losing valuable time. The techniques given in this course will also help to minimize this problem.

Another habit most readers have is subvocalizing, or silently pronouncing each and every word to themselves. This is mentally translating the written symbols to verbal ones. By saying each word silently, you tie yourself closely to your rate of speech. You can go somewhat faster, of course, because your lips don't move, but this still wastes time and effort. If you just try to stop doing this, you'll find it difficult, but the techniques you'll learn here do the job naturally and automatically while you actually are reading. You should know that no one ever completely stops subvocalizing, but you will find yourself doing it less and less over the next 30 days.

Since these habits were fixed at an early age, they've become so much a part of you that now you are comfortable only when reading this "old" way. These "bad" habits are ingrained into your reading patterns. We might say you have been "programmed" with them.

Through education and practice, you have been "programmed" to read a certain way and it's become as comfortable as a pair of old slippers. The only problem with this is that most readers are stuck in these habits and, therefore, have only one basic method and speed for reading everything. They must read and study important material the same way they read the comics section of the newspaper.

Deprogramming Yourself

I am going to show you how to "deprogram" yourself over the next month. Then, instead of being the effect of your reading habits, you can begin to take charge over them. This does not mean you cannot read your old way; it means you will not be forced by habit and a lack of skills to read the old way only. You're adding some new tools to your reading tool kit. You'll always reach for the old familiar ones until you become used to the new ones. Then you'll pick the best tool for the job.

Through years of researching various reading improvement tools, I have eliminated the unnecessary ones and brought together the most simple, natural and effective techniques. You'll discover some of these techniques used in courses that cost from hundreds to thousands of dollars, but they are used differently. I believe, for the most part, that they are not evaluated properly or taught as effectively as possible. A student may temporarily be pushed faster, but is likely to fall back.

In this course, you will steadily and gradually build your skills. You won't be pushed faster than you can read and comprehend.

Even at the risk of being overly repetitious, I must remind you once again that your real gain will come from doing this course as laid out and using the techniques. There simply is no escape from this fact. Doing it is what will do it for you, and doing it gradually will do it best.

If you give the mind an easy task to do on a conscious level, it will handle the difficult tasks at the subconscious level. In other words, by consciously using your finger or regulator when you read, you will stop regressing automatically and you naturally will begin to read several words at a time. Eventually you will hear them less and less. A similar approach is used in many other educational endeavors.

Maximum Benefit

If you wish to get the maximum benefit from this course, you must use your finger, pencil or pen as much as possible during the next 30 days. <u>This is a key point; use your regulator to underline as much as you can.</u>

Remember, I'm not asking you to read faster or to comprehend less. Read for the same level of comprehension you always have. Don't worry about your speed because it will increase as you drop your bad habits and begin to utilize your natural abilities. <u>Simply underline everything as you read.</u>

If you notice you're not comprehending, stop, go back and reread; do not continue going over the words without understanding them. While many people do this and call it reading, we know it is merely a waste of time. Always make sure you get what you want from the material. Anything else just isn't reading.

Another excellent method of checking your comprehension is to have someone else read the same passage and then discuss it with you. Refer back to the passage to check any questions or differences. Never worry about who is right or wrong; concentrate on getting better through more practice. You will always want to go back and reread it afterwards to check for yourself, even if you both agree on the content. This will give you the most certainty and confidence in your ability to comprehend.

During this first week, quiz and check yourself on many types of material. Question your assumptions about what things mean and what you're reading. Do you really understand it? Do you want to? Are you really getting what you need and want? Check back in a few days or a week. How much have you forgotten? How much have you remembered? Don't ever be disappointed because you will steadily improve with practice.

Already you may have wondered if you'll need to read with a regulator for the rest of your life. No, you won't. This is merely a tool we'll use to exercise and expand your reading abilities. However, you may find it so helpful for speed and concentration that you will always use it to some extent. This is up to you.

During this coming week, if you get to a point where using your finger bothers you too much to continue, then stop using it for awhile. Read without it for a time. At some later point, start again, although now I suggest you switch to a pen or pencil. This procedure, repeated as necessary, will handle almost any discomfort you may have.

As with all learning experiences, you'll hit plateaus of performance. You'll be increasing right along and then, no more gain. This is only temporary. You will improve more as long as you continue to exercise and use the techniques. Some people find it most helpful to increase the amount they practice until they "break through" the level at which they're stuck. You may try this if you wish, but don't worry. Plateaus are to be expected. Unless you decide to stay on one, you'll soon leave it behind.

Well, that's it for this lesson, except that you should do the first week's exercise now to try it out. Concentrate on comprehension this week, speed next week.

And remember: use your regulator, be it finger, pen or pencil.

Chapter 10

1st Week's Exercises

Every day for the next 7 days use the regulating technique as much as you can on everything you read. Also use your preview step.

You'll notice that I have given you a choice of 5 paths through this course. No matter how you feel about reading, one of these paths will suit you.

Path 1

You wish to do this course as recommended for your maximum gain. This week you're going to work on comprehension and speed.

If you already read more than 15 minutes daily, you should begin doing this exercise at least once each day. Doing this exercise more than once a day is optional, but it will help you to attain your goal more quickly. And keep track of your practice by filling in your daily log.

1st Week's Exercise

1. Set aside 15 minutes to read.
2. Read for 10 minutes using your "regulator."
3. Reread this same material with comprehension in 5 minutes, still using your regulator. Look for new ideas you missed on your first reading. If you can't complete the whole section in the 5 minutes, that's all right. Just do your best.
4. Use your regulator on most everything you read.
5. Fill in your log daily.

Don't worry about people making jokes, laughing or teasing you; see what they say in 30 days. Read anything you wish, particularly things that interest you. Enjoy yourself and read a lot.

Supplemental Reading

I also recommend that this week you read *Animal Farm* by George Orwell, Signet Classic, New York, 1996. This classic of political satire clearly demonstrates the importance of reading for a free society.

Path 2

You've found that it bothers you too much to use a regulator most of the time.

Then use a regulator (I suggest a ballpoint pen, capped) only during the 5-minute portion of Exercise 1 and when convenient, as you read daily. But, you must realize that your final results may be less and may take longer to achieve.

Path 3

You've decided to wait awhile before doing this course. Maybe it looks a little harder than you thought it would be or you may not wish to do it just now. Perhaps it bothers you too much to use a regulator when you read or causes you some discomfort. That's all right; you can still benefit.

Over the next two weeks, use a regulator intermittently. Never use it for more than 2 to 4 minutes at a stretch and even a few seconds is okay.

In two weeks, check your reading again. When you wish, begin to Preview occasionally. Finally, whenever you're ready, switch to Path 2 or Path 1.

Path 4

If you don't like to read, ignore everything I've said up to now.

Obviously you can go on in the future as you've done in the past. However, stop and think about this. Since the invention of writing, positions of authority, responsibility and worth have increasingly depended on the single skill of reading. Writing and mathematics follow closely behind, and this is true for all civilizations and history.

You needn't be filled totally with pain, however. Reading more effectively makes reading more fun. And the way to learn to read more effectively is to have some fun reading. Go read, and read anything that interests you, but read. Start with newspapers and read things that catch your eye at first. *Later, you can cover it all.*

Magazines. Read any of them; look at the pictures. Question if what they say is true. Do the same with newspapers. You'll find the answer on one page or another, or later in a book.

Talk to your librarian and find out what is in the library that is of interest to you. Soon you'll begin to enjoy reading, and nicest surprise of all, you'll be ready to read anything.

How long is soon? That's up to you. It could be as short as two months or as long as two years. But you can get there, even if you need some tutoring or help along the way.

When you enjoy reading, you're definitely ready for Path 3 if you haven't already started it.

Path 5

Follow any of the paths above, but substitute the following books for your weekly supplemental reading.

Path 5 Books

Lesson I – 1st Week Suggested Reading

Animal Farm by George Orwell, Signet Classic, New York, 1996.

Mosaic of Thought: Teaching Comprehension in a Readers's Workshop by Ellin Oliver Keen and Susan Zimmermann, Heinemann Publishing, New Hampshire, 1997.

Lesson II – 2nd Week Suggested Reading

A History of Reading by Alberto Manguel, Penguin Books, New York, 1997.

How to Read and Why by Harold Bloom, Scribner, New York, 2001.

Mapping the Mind by Rita Carter, University of California Press, Berkeley, California, 1999.

Lesson III – 3rd Week Suggested Reading

The World's Religions: Our Great Wisdom Traditions by Huston Smith, Harper Collins Publishers Inc., New York, 1991.

The Astonishing Hypothesis: The Scientific Search for the Soul by Francis Crick, Simon & Shuster, New York, 1994.

Understanding Reading: A Psycholinguistic Analysis of Reading and Learning to Read, 5th Ed. by Frank Smith, Lawrence Erlbaum Associates, Inc., New Jersey, 1994.

Lesson IV – 4th Week Suggested Reading

Consilience: The Unity of Knowledge by Edward O. Wilson, Vintage Books, New York, 1998.

Billions and Billions: Thoughts on Life and Death at the Brink of the Millenium by Carl Sagan, Random House, New York, 1997.

The Wealth and Poverty of Nations: Why Some Are So Rich And Some So Poor by David S. Landes, W.W. Norton & Company, New York 1999.

The Elegant Universe: Superstrings, Hidden Dimensions and the Quest for the Ultimate Theory by Brian Greene, Vintage Books, New York, 2000.

Note

If you already are reading above 350 wpm and have little need to improve your comprehension, then please note this carefully: you do not have to spend a full week on Lesson I; you may move on to Lesson II in a couple of days or as soon as you wish. However, it is vitally important that you spend two weeks using the procedures given in these two lessons. You may try any and all of the information in the course as you wish, but remember the maximum benefit will come from doing this course as laid out.

Log 1st Week

1st Day:

Today I read_____
(name of book or type of material)

for_____
(amount of time)

2nd Day:

Today I read_____

for_____

3rd Day:

Today I read_____

for_____

4th Day:

Today I read_____

for_____

5th Day:

Today I read_____

for_____

6th Day:

Today I read_____

for_____

7th Day:

Today I read_____

for_____

Remember, you must do it to get it!

2nd WEEK – LESSON II

Knowledge and human power are synonymous.
Francis Bacon

Chapter 11

Increasing Your Speed

Welcome back. I hope you enjoyed this past week and made some progress toward your goals. If you felt it was a tough week, take heart. It was one of the roughest, but things will get easier.

This week we are going to begin to work more on your speed, take a closer look at perception and see how Power Reading works.

Speed

We'll start with your speed. By now you're used to the jokes and strange looks you get when you read "like a kid," using your finger or regulator. More importantly, you've probably noticed you had trouble at times keeping your regulator up with your reading rate. If so, you may have already progressed to this next step on your own.

This next step is to shorten the distance your regulator (finger, pen or pencil) travels so it covers only 2/3 to 1/2 of the actual line. You still see and read every word, of course.

Shortened Underlining

This week will basically be a continuation of last week's lesson. We will cover new ground and further the discussion of reading that we began last week. In these first two weeks, it is important that we reemphasize comprehension, because it is the most fundamental of all your reading tools.

Once you know you are getting what you want and need from your reading, then you can begin to work on your speed. The first step is your preview. While this technique helps comprehension, it also improves speed of reading. As soon as you know what the material is about and what its conclusions are, you can speed your travel down the path the author presents. As you note the facts given, the references cited and the arguments set forth, you will form your own opinions of the author's conclusions.

Soon, if not already, you will find yourself less willing to accept everything immediately and more inclined to think about it for yourself first. Education means "to lead out," and it almost always leads to thinking for yourself. This independence of mind has given us change and progress throughout history. A large part of it comes from comprehending what earlier people have written; thus, our stress on comprehension before speed.

Your regulator will do less and your eyes will do more. Let this occur naturally, and do not try to push yourself too fast. Read for comprehension and don't worry. Your speed will continue to improve as you do your daily exercises.

Understanding

As you read, be sure you see and understand every word, even though your fingers aren't underlining those words on the far left and far right of the line. As you begin to read faster, you still want full comprehension. It won't do you much good to start skipping over words. One of them may be a "not" that could result in your reversing the author's message.

The way to prevent this error is not to keep asking yourself: "Did I see every word?" Just be sure you are comfortably understanding what the author says. Let comfort be your guide. If you are following right along, then you are usually doing just fine.

If you begin to go too fast and get a little confused or lost, then go back to where you were doing well. Come forward again and straighten yourself out. Then continue on.

There is no substitute for comprehension. It is up to you to ensure that you get it because no one else can do it for you. Your two keys are comfort and understanding.

If you feel you are comfortable with what the author is

saying and you are understanding him easily, then you are all right. Of course, you have to use good judgment and common sense. There are exceptions to every rule, but this is a good basic one to follow.

At times you may be unfamiliar with the author's subject matter. In this case, you may not obtain a full understanding at first and will need to work harder to grasp what is being said. Sometimes an author will invent terms or use them in her own manner. If she doesn't define them for you immediately, you may have to keep on reading or jump ahead to find the definitions she gives and uses. This is not too helpful to the reader, nor is it particularly good writing, but when it is done, you can handle it in this way. Then there are authors who do not write clearly or concisely or logically. These also make for needlessly difficult reading.

Fortunately, these cases are exceptions to the rule, so you shouldn't blame all your problems on the author. However, if most everything you read seems this way to you, then you need to move to easier materials for awhile and gradually build up your reading vocabulary and skills. The easiest way to improve your reading is not to struggle endlessly with a single book that is too difficult for you. Go out and find several that are interesting and easy. Have fun and enjoy yourself at first before picking up more difficult books and working your way up gradually. Finally, you will find yourself breezing through books which earlier you would have dreaded and avoided because they were too difficult.

It is probably apparent to you by now that speed and comprehension are intertwined. As you read better, you will be able to read faster. Speed is not a substitute for comprehension, but they both can improve together. The best way is to let speed increase gradually and naturally while you ensure you understand what you read.

Once again, we are going to shift from this book to some material of your own choosing. I want you to use this shortened underlining or regulating technique for 5 minutes or so in some other material.

Read for 5 Minutes in Material of Your Choice Using the Shortened Regulating Technique

Did you notice any difference? Did you find it easier? Were you able to move over the material with less effort? Did you make sure that you still understood what you were reading? If the answers to these questions were yes, then you are ready to continue. If they were no, then you should spend more time using this shortened technique until the answers are yes. Then you will be ready to continue. This shortened technique will help you read faster naturally. The more you use it, the sooner you will become used to it and begin to see an improvement.

We will not, however, be reading the same way all the time. At times, I will give you exercises or drills that place little or no emphasis on comprehension. These are designed to work with your perception faculties. Before you can understand the material, you need to perceive it. So let's take a look at perception as it pertains to your reading.

Chapter 12

Perception

Reading starts with visual perception. This process begins with energy in the form of light rays. The light rays are emitted from a natural source such as the sun or from artificial sources such as fluorescent or incandescent lamps. These rays are reflected off the page and go into your eye where they form an image.

The Eye

The iris is the colored portion of your eye, and the pupil is the black part in the middle of it. By contracting or expanding, the iris regulates the amount of light that can come into your eye. Under the pupil, the lens focuses the light rays into an image on the back wall of the eyeball, the retina.

In some ways the eye resembles a camera. The iris acts as a shutter to control the amount of light that enters the eye, and the lens serves, as it does in a camera, to focus the image. Structurally, the eye is far more complex. In a camera, the lens is moved toward the film or away from it in order to focus the image. In the eye, the lens' shape is actually changed by tiny muscles directed by the brain. They squeeze or expand, and the lens changes shape in order to focus the image on the retina.

Hundreds of other small muscles control the turning of the eyes, the lens action and the contraction or expansion of the iris. All of these work in harmony to let the right amount of light in and to focus the image on the retina.

The retina itself consists of millions of light-sensitive cells. There are approximately 127 million, and each one responds individually to light. There are 2 basic types named for their shape: rods and cones. The rods far outnumber the cones, approximately 120 million to 7 million, and they differ in function.

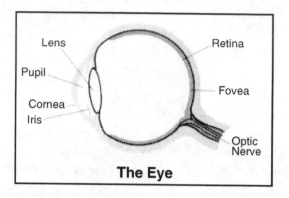

The Eye

The rods are not color sensitive, the cones are. The rods register only black, white and shades of gray, no color. Thus, they are effective at night when there is no color to see. The cones are concentrated at the fovea, the "center" of the retina, and the point where an image is focused. There are fewer cones as you move away from the fovea toward the extremities of the retina.

At the point of focus, the fovea, there are no rods. They are distributed throughout the retina, although they too are packed more closely near the center. When the sun goes down, there is not enough light to stimulate the cones, so you see only black and light and various shades of gray. This is possible because there still is enough light to stimulate the rods. The rods are capable of detecting motion, but not seeing color or focusing sharply. This is why you can see things at night from the corner of your eye that you would miss otherwise.

There are neither rods nor cones at the spot where the optic nerve joins the retina. The optic nerve takes the eye's messages and transmits them to the brain. This connection to the retina causes a "blind spot" in your field of vision. You're not normally aware of this spot, because you can't "see" it and your brain "fills in" the information in its mental picture, but it's there.

Blind Spot

Cover left eye, stare at cross and move the book back and forth until "R" disappears (usually 8-12 inches). For opposite eye, turn book upside down.

The most important fact here is that you see in two ways. Primarily, you see or focus with the cones. These are concentrated where the image is focused at the retina. Whatever you focus upon is what you are most conscious of seeing, but that's not all you "see." You "see" at two levels simultaneously. You consciously see what you are focusing on now and subconsciously what you are going to focus on next.

Your eyes can focus only when they are at rest. This is called a "fixation." While your eyes move from one fixation point to another, you see nothing. No information can be registered while your eyes shift, only while they are still.

Thus, your vision of the world comes from a series of individual fixations. The eye comes to a stop, focuses and registers the information on the retina. This fixation only takes an instant, and then it is immediately followed by another, and so on. This process is entirely automatic. What you "see" is sort of a series of still pictures or snapshots. These come in and are integrated into a moving whole by the brain, but each piece of the moving picture is a single frame. This is similar to a movie film which also consists of a series of individual picture frames. When you see one after another rapidly, you see motion because they come too quickly in succession for the eye and brain to distinguish them individually.

Look around the room for a minute. You will notice you can see even while you are looking around. But how can this be? It is because your eyes stop, focus and register an image much faster than you consciously realize. The moving images you see mentally come from the integration of this series of fixations. There is no vision in between. It's fast. Your eye must stop and focus for about 1/4 of a second for an image to register on the retina. It is constantly moving and stopping. It oscillates at least 4 times a second. This eye motion is called saccadic movement from the French saccade — to jerk.

The eye moves to a fixation point, fixates, the information comes in and then the eye moves to the next fixation point.

The Brain

How does the eye know what to focus on next? It doesn't, but it is directed by the brain which does know. The brain not only receives what you consciously "see," but also subconsciously receives what is outside the immediate area of focus. With this information, the brain determines what to focus on next. This is how you can react to something coming into your field of vision before you actually focus on and consciously see it. Many people have flinched from a ball, rock, or other projectile coming from outside their normal field of vision and have been saved from harm by this mechanism. You see at both levels.

As you read, the brain determines what you need to see next in order to continue your understanding. Using this information, it then directs your eyes to the next piece of data you need, and so you advance step-by-step. This same process is utilized whether you are sweeping your eyes across the horizon, a room or a sentence. These mechanisms are entirely automatic and below your level of conscious control.

Consciously, you pick the goal. You decide what you

want to see, read and understand, and the brain automatically carries out a fantastic number of steps to achieve this goal.

But, this isn't all there is to your perception. The focusing and moving of your eyes are just a start. You end up seeing a single picture, but it is made up of of several parts.

There are more than six neural interchanges between the eye and the brain. Between the retina and the optic nerve alone there is a great transformation. The data from 127 million cells must be compressed into one million nerve pathways. This information, now condensed to less than 1/100th of what it was, is transmitted along the optic nerve to the brain. Finally, all of the information is subconsciously pieced together to form the single picture that you consciously see.

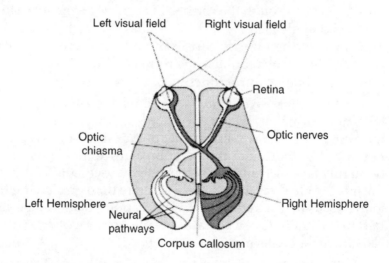

Brain-Vision Interaction

Information from the left side of each eye goes to the left hemisphere. Thus, it "sees" the right visual field and controls the right side of the body. The opposite occurs for the other side.

How this picture is integrated and how you "see" it mentally is still a mystery to the scientific world, but bits and pieces of the process are understood. Most functions of the left side of the body — left hand, left foot, etc. — are controlled by the right side of the brain, or the right hemisphere. The other side of the body, the right side, is controlled by the left side of the brain. Thus, if a person suffers a stroke and the left side of the body is paralyzed, it is because the other side of the brain, the right hemisphere, has been damaged.

Vision is different, however. It is not a simple crossover. The right sides of the images from both eyes go to the brain's right hemisphere. The left sides of the images from both eyes go to the left hemisphere. These sides or hemispheres can function independently, but all this information is integrated somehow (possibly through the connecting corpus callosum) so that we "see" a single picture. No one yet knows exactly how this is done or how the information from both hemispheres is collated and integrated, but it appears to be different than many other brain-body control functions.

Then there is another factor: time. We already know it takes approximately 1/4 of a second for an image to register on the retina. This image will fade or "decay" in 1/2 to 1 second if nothing else comes into the eye. You can see this for yourself by staring at something, then closing your eyes and watching the image fade away. But "seeing" is more than just having the image focus on the retina. The information must then be carried to the brain, registered and grasped or processed. This is called your short-term memory.

It takes approximately 1/4 of a second for a complete short-term memory cycle to occur. During this brief time, the information comes into your short-term memory, registers, then fades out. As it fades, the brain gets ready to accept more data, and the process repeats itself. The process works similarly for things that you hear, touch, etc.

This process of "seeing" is a complex one. It takes place through the integrated combination of conscious and subconscious perception. There are hundreds of steps in the process and billions of cells involved. It is difficult to isolate and work on an individual step in the process, because all the parts of the process must function together for words to be perceived and read.

Some courses try to isolate and work on individual parts of the perception process. We shall look at them, their techniques and machines in the next chapter. But, no matter what methods are used to increase reading speed, some data indicate there is an upper limit.

Calculating the time for the image to register, the number of words clearly seen, the time for the eyes to move to a new fixation point, and so on, various experts have concluded that the upper limit to reading speed is about 900 words per minute. Anything faster than this means that you must skip some words; it is "skimming" for the key words or main ideas or "scanning" for answers to specific questions. Since you do not have time to see each word clearly above 900 wpm, and if reading is defined as seeing and registering each word clearly, you cannot "read" faster than this.

However, since this is about 4 times faster than the average reader reads, it allows a great deal of room for improvement. In certain types of material that are simple or familiar to the reader, it may be possible to go even faster. To skim faster is not too difficult, but to read faster is exceptional. Even so, 900 wpm is 2 to 4 pages per minute in most books. Not a bad rate for an "average" reader.

There is much skepticism in the academic community concerning claims of speedreading courses which advertise that their students end up reading thousands or tens of thousands of words per minute. Later we shall see a possible explanation for how some people might be able to do this, but studies show that such claims are outside the range of average readers. There appears to be an upper limit for most people and the 900 wpm plateau seems to be it. You may be one of the exceptions, but even if you are not, a speed of 900 wpm would put you among the world's fastest readers.

This discussion of perception is here for more than just to have you practice reading for comprehension. Now you can see how many things have to happen before you can even perceive words, much less read and understand them. Reading starts as perception, but ends up as thought, and you cannot read faster than you can think. Not only does the information have to come in and be registered, but it must be digested and assimilated to be understood. This is an individual matter. Each individual has his own rate and upper limit for thinking and reading.

Looking at how high this upper limit is, you might well wonder why people read so slowly. We've discussed this briefly, but now let's examine it in more detail.

Chapter 13

Why You Read the Way You Do

Learning to speak precedes learning to read, thus, someone learning to read knows what a word "means" when he hears it. In teaching a child to read, it is typical to have him either sound out the word so he can understand it (the phonic method) or recognize it all at once and associate the whole word with its sound and meaning (whole word recognition). These are called the phonic or code method and the whole word recognition or analytic method. They are the two basic methods for teaching reading. The explanations given here are simplified, but they cover the range of basic reading instruction.

It's interesting that after more than 100 years of study and research, no conclusive results have been reached as to which method is better. Both systems, or a combination, can produce good results, but no single "best" method to teach children to read has been developed yet.

Some data show that children below the fourth grade level may learn better using a phonic system at first, but above this level, a whole word recognition approach seems to be more effective. However, the evidence is not conclusive, and other factors may be equally or more important.

How much time does the teacher have available to work with the individual student? How many students are there in the class? Does the child have to struggle to keep up with the class pace? What is the home atmosphere like, and do the parents read much? Do they enjoy reading? Do the parents spend time reading with their child? How much? How is the TV used at home? The answers to these questions are the most important factors in establishing a healthy reading environment.

Many children never read beyond what they must for

school, and it is no wonder they often end up hating reading. Some get stuck in the comic book stage and never get out. Comic books are excellent tools as long as they are part of a program designed to take the child above the comic book level to other types of reading material. Adventure books, age-level magazines and stories would be an appropriate next level.

Far too many children never are asked what they are really interested in and then directed to materials in those areas at their level. In some cases, students must be individually helped until they can enjoy reading on their own. Volunteer tutorial programs are helping in this area and have proven effective. The most important factors overall are individual attention, interesting materials and working at the child's own level.

Mental Dictionary

When a child can look at words and work out the sounds, another factor comes into play. Just as each of us has a visual map of the world inside our heads, we each have a mental working dictionary. This is our "map" for reading; it is automatically consulted and tells us what each word means.

The meanings of the words we use every day were established as we learned to speak. Thus, whatever the word meant to our mother, father, brothers, sisters, grandparents, friends and others around us, it usually meant the same to us. This would be the word's correct meaning within the community where it's used, but it may not be the correct meaning in the outside world. The meaning of the word as we've been taught to use it may encompass only a portion of the actual meaning. It may be partially incorrect, entirely incorrect, or even, in extreme cases, the opposite.

This is why many experts consider it important to study and understand the complete meaning of words, including their history or etymology. They consider a full understanding of fewer words to be a better basis for reading than an incomplete, partial understanding of many words. As in most things, there are experts who feel just the opposite, and the common sense approach lies somewhere in between.

An interesting study of successful corporate executives in the United States revealed one common trait. These executives came from all types of economic backgrounds, from rich to poor. Some had college degrees and others did not, and some scored high on IQ tests and others did poorly. None of these factors was the same for all. What they did have in common were outstanding vocabularies. Usually these came from reading widely.

Should you then go out and begin memorizing the dictionary? Perhaps, but it isn't necessary. There's a much easier, more natural way to improve your vocabulary. . . read more! And as you read, stop and look up any questionable words. This is the most natural approach for improving your vocabulary, and the results last far longer than dull memorizations of word lists.

There are many meanings for most words, and you should use each word you look up in several sentences until you can use it comfortably. As we will learn when we cover study techniques, if you don't use the information, you are very likely to lose it. Using a word in sentences will help both your understanding and retention of it.

Reading itself is a linear progression; it follows step-by-step. If you miss one step or take it in a slightly different direction, you can go off the path and soon find yourself lost in the woods. This can happen frequently if you misconstrue the meanings of words, and it is why many people lose comprehension when they're reading.

Another reason for poor reading is that many people read so slowly they have a difficult time remembering what the author is talking about. They cannot see the forest because they are lost amongst the trees. This is because of their short-term memory. The 4 to 7 items that short-term memory can hold fade out quickly. Thus, they cannot remember the beginning of the line by the time they get to the end of it. Literally, they often bore themselves by getting stuck looking at individual words and sentences. This will be handled by Looking at the Whole, Your Approach and Regulating yourself.

But these are not the only reasons some readers read slowly. There are many others. We have seen how your eye takes in information when it stops or fixates. The amount of information it takes in is determined by your span of perception.

Your span of perception is how much of a line of print you can see with a single fixation. Average readers see only a few letters or syllables each time they fixate.

You can see this illustrated on the next page.

Average Reader

Another reason for poor reading is that many people read so

slowly they have a difficult time remembering what the

author is talking about. They cannot see the forest because

they are lost among the trees. Literally they often bore

/___/\\ = Denotes one fixation

Thus, they cannot read as rapidly as readers who see whole words and phrases.

Efficient Reader

Another reason for poor reading is that many people read so

slowly they have a difficult time remembering what the

author is talking about. They cannot see the forest because

they are lost among the trees. Literally they often bore

/___/\\ = Denotes one fixation

Your perception span has inherent limits, but few readers utilize their capabilities to increase it. You are already doing so now.

It is being improved through your use of the regulator. This increases your span of perception, because as you read faster, your eyes are forced by necessity to see more with each fixation.

At the same time, the use of your regulator helps reduce your regressions. Regressions are the backward glances or fixations toward the left instead of the right. Some readers spend up to 50 percent of their reading time actually going backward over what they've already seen and read. That means they are "reading" only half the time they think they are!

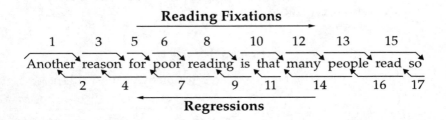

You can see the path of reading fixations illustrated in another way by the example on the next page.

1. Another
   2. -her rea-
      3. reason
         4. -son for
            5. for
               6. poor
                  7. poor read-
                     8. reading
                        9. -ing is
                           10. is that
                              11. that
                                 12.many
                                    13. people
                                       14. many peo-
                                          15. read so
                                             16. -ple read
                                                17. so

Fixations For Reading

Your eyes do not always move forward in a straight, fixed pattern. Directed by the brain, they jump around to get the information necessary for you to see and understand what you are trying to read. When you first began to learn to read, you were uncertain what the words meant and naturally looked back to check yourself and make sure of what you read. Most readers continue this habit at a subconscious level even though it is no longer necessary and actually slows them down.

Regulating yourself as you read will also help you to overcome this habit. The nature of eyesight functioning always causes some leftward movement, but it will be naturally reduced to a minimum.

There is yet another factor that slows up many readers. This is subvocalizaton or saying the words to yourself as you read. It, too, is a holdover from when you first learned to read. The rate at which you speak affects the rate at which you read. Since the average person talks at a rate of 120 – 150 words per minute, this will tend to keep her reading speed slowed down.

Readers who read less than 150 wpm often still move their lips, tongue and vocal cords; some actually pronounce the words aloud, more or less softly, as they read. These are often called "lip" readers. These readers still are doing what they learned when they began reading and haven't progressed beyond this point. They can be given gum to chew to keep their lips busy, but reading a great deal of fairly easy material is their best program, and after they begin to read faster, this habit will disappear.

The next stage is no longer moving the lips, tongue and vocal cords, but still saying each word silently inside your head. Because you aren't physically moving these body parts, your speed will be somewhat faster, but it is still tied to your rate of speech. Most readers are at this point.

As you begin to read above 350 wpm, you simply don't have time to say every word. Many small and less important words no longer are heard, although they still are seen and understood. You will begin to hear fewer words and to receive ideas and impressions more directly as you read faster.

Above 550 wpm you are picking up only a few key words and phrases at a subvocal level. There is simply not enough time, even mentally, to say every word.

You do not need to worry about this process; it occurs as you learn to read faster. What happens is that your subconscious reading habits readjust gradually as you have less and less time to hear every word because of your faster reading speed. The key to this process is a gradual transition from old habits to new ones. The regulator is the tool that helps you make the transition.

As you can see, using your finger, pen or pencil as a regulator has many advantages that help make it the best method for increasing reading speed and effectiveness.

Chapter 14

Changing Your Habits

How and why are your habits changing?

Some courses use machines and specialized materials to try to change your habits. We'll briefly discuss some of these techniques and compare them to ours. Among those we'll discuss are the tachistoscope, controlled pacing machines, motion pictures, filmstrips, narrow-columned materials that progressively widen, flash cards and simple books with large print.

The tachistoscope is a machine that functions in some respects as a slide projector does. It flashes words quickly on a screen, acting as sort of a mechanical flash card. With it, the student can work at and practice quick recognition of letters, words and phrases. The machines range from a simple flash card design to expensive, complicated ones that have accurate timing devices for controlling the exact exposure.

The purpose of this device is twofold. First, it gives you practice in fixating more quickly, thus allowing you to approach the minimum of 1/16th of a second to see a word instead of the four times slower fixation rate of the average reader of 1/4th of a second. Theoretically, this would allow you to read 4 times faster. This machine was used during World War II to train spotters and pilots to recognize and react quickly to silhouettes of enemy planes and ships.

Its second purpose is to get the reader to see whole words and, later, phrases in a single fixation. Usually these are flashed on a screen in front of a student or class by a projection tachistoscope and followed by tests given to check comprehension. The tests are supposed to motivate the student to comprehend better.

While students may become very accurate at reading isolated words and phrases on a screen, when they turn to their books, there are no such artificial divisions among the words and phrases. There is no machine to separate the words in space and time for them. As a result, there is usually a limited benefit transferred to the actual reading process, because old habits tend to reassert themselves.

Reading is a continuous process of seeing and understanding new words in light of what you already have read. You do not glimpse single words out of context. More importantly, it takes about 1/4th of a second for the entire process of cycling information into your short-term memory, recognizing it and having it clear out for the next batch of information. A bottleneck is created in the process if the eyes are trying to take in information faster than the mind can grasp its meaning.

It is nearly impossible to single out a portion of the whole, balanced process of reading because it is so interrelated and complex. Because this integrated relationship works primarily at the subconscious level, it is improved best when you work on the whole system in a natural setting.

As with most skills, when you wish to improve them, you should do so gradually. Trying to rush the process can lead to frustration, disappointment and failure.

Controlled reading pacers are machines designed to push you at a steady, predetermined rate. Some of the more expensive ones allow you to vary the rate with the use of a speed control device that works like a foot pedal on a sewing machine. Controlled pacers also come in various designs. These include slide projector types, overhead projectors, motion pictures and a simple bar shaped like a "T" pushed by a small electric motor that slides it down the page, forcing you to cover the material at the machine's pace.

Controlled reading pacers can take up where the tachistoscopes leave off. Some of them project line-by-line on a projection screen or a smaller TV-type screen. They roll the print or material along at a steady rate, forcing the reader to keep up. If you fall behind this machine, you can encounter the same kind of frustration that occurs when trying to take dictation and falling hopelessly behind. Few of the machines can slow up. They do not allow you to reread when you wish, and your comprehension can falter. This is one of the difficulties with them. If the reader falls behind in comprehension, he must skip ahead or be lost.

The purpose of these mechanical pacers is twofold. They force you to read faster, and secondly, they prevent you from regressing. These are widely used in various reading improvement programs across the country. Unfortunately, they also lack much permanent carryover into the students' actual reading materials. Why is this?

Ideas are not distributed evenly throughout written material. Sometimes one idea is spread across 10 pages, and at other times there are 10 separate ideas placed together on a single page. Some ideas are more important or are more complicated than others and must be read several times and thought through. There may be words to look up, which requires stopping. These factors all are integral to the reading process. Simply seeing words faster without understanding them is not reading. It doesn't mean it should never be done, but it must be done in the proper context, as we shall see.

Another teaching device for improving reading speed is the use of narrow specialized materials. They usually start out with a column width of one or two words and then expand as the reader progresses.

Another
teaching device
for improving reading
speed is the use of narrow
specialized materials.They usually
start out with a column width of one or two
words and then expand as the reader progresses.

Narrow Columns

These can be presented in special workbooks, on cards, in motion pictures and on filmstrips or continuous rolls. Often they present a story or article. This is another method of trying to expand the span of perception. As usually happens when you try to improve just one part of the reading process, it is not universally successful, although it too can be helpful. Newspaper columns will also help.

In this course, as you use a regulator, your eyes, directed by the brain, do these same things automatically as you begin to read faster. When you work to improve your reading as a whole, the working of each portion of the process improves in a balanced, natural fashion. Each part works much more efficiently at a subconscious level to produce the conscious goal. Concentration on a part at a time doesn't easily, effectively carry over to the whole process of reading.

This is not to say that machines and specialized materials are completely without value. In fact, they can be helpful. But the techniques used in this course perform the same functions more effectively.

Using your finger, pen or pencil as a regulator serves as a handy adjustable tool for improving reading. A few people feel it just gets in the way, but most find it tends to speed up the reading process. You are visibly conscious of the rate at which you read. Rereading becomes a conscious decision and can be done as desired. You can easily stop and look up the meanings of words and use your own material. Speeding up and slowing down are readily apparent and easily controlled. These are key factors.

As you read faster, you naturally will begin to see more with each fixation. Subvocalization drops out a bit at a time as your speed gradually increases. And as time goes on, you will begin to get impressions and ideas more directly. It will take work and practice, but you can do it.

Another of the keys is to read more. Read whatever interests you. Go to the library and ask the librarian for some good books in your favorite areas. Abundant help and materials are waiting for you to take advantage of them. In some cases, students have improved as much from simply reading more as they have from taking conventional speedreading courses. You'll get the maximum benefit if you both read more and use the techniques given in this course.

Usually you will not use a regulator when reading on a computer screen, although many people find it helpful to use the mouse cursor as a regulator. However, you should occasionally do one of the daily drills using the computer so you can see how fast you are reading on it and drill at a faster rate.

Chapter 15

Reading Various Types of Materials

Up to now we have looked at reading in general. The entire process has been our subject. No specific reference has been made to reading a particular type of material or how this affects the reading process.

The varieties of reading materials are enormous. There are newspapers, magazines, journals, monographs, short stories, novellas, novels, poems, plays, documents, transcripts and books covering an immense range of data, information, facts and theory. Of course, this barely scratches the surface. The entire range of human knowledge, experience and wisdom is contained in written form.

All written forms are not the same, nor do they all use an alphabet that represents sounds. There are other types of symbology or writing. In the past, for example in Egypt, pictographic writing was used. Pictures were the symbols that had meaning instead of the letters and words in use today. Each

Egyptian hieroglyphics on wall behind figures in foreground.

picture, or hieroglyphic, had its own meaning or definition. These hieroglyphics were as communicative as the symbols we use today, and some feel they were more beautiful.

Millions of people around the world today still write in ancient, artistic forms. Among these are the ideographic characters currently used by the Chinese, Japanese and Koreans. In ideographic forms, various symbols stand for ideas or objects. For example, a circle could represent the sun, day, light or warmth. Thus, the symbol directly represents the idea rather than a sound.

More familiar to us is the symbol system used in music. Mathematics also has its own set of symbols as do many other branches of knowledge. There is an advantage to this. The ideas can be condensed and made so specific and exact that what would take a great number of words to express to the layman can be expressed in only a few symbols to another "fluent" in the language — an "expert."

New Languages

Specialization and the virtual explosion of knowledge have led to the development of numerous special terms in all fields. Often a term will have a special meaning within the context of a certain field of study, and the same word may mean something entirely different to the general public.

This is one of the difficulties in reading in an unfamiliar subject. Literally, it is a new language for you. To compound this difficulty, changes and discoveries are occurring so rapidly today that most specialty languages are constantly evolving. Thus, one must keep current to remain fluent. For someone who has been absent from a field for 10 years, this can present a considerable problem.

None of this is insurmountable, but it does complicate the process of reading, especially technical material. As we know, if you don't know the meaning of the words or symbols, you won't understand what you see. And if you merely go over words and symbols without comprehending, you are not really reading. Here, the problem gives us our solution: once again you must look up the words, terms and symbols, and make sure you understand them.

Approaching any subject for the first time can be a bewildering experience. There seems to be a mountain of complexity, the summit and mastery of which at first appears to be insurmountable. Yet, after a great deal of step-by-step effort and persistence, you can find yourself at the top one day. Then the subject will not seem too difficult; it may even seem simple. What's happened? Through study and usage, the mass of terms has become part of your "everyday" vocabulary. The principles that underlie the subject become logical, straightforward, and finally, part of your common sense and thinking. But all of this happens only with time and after you have had enough experience using the subject.

Experience

Experience is the key. You get experience from exposure to, and working with, a subject. You approach any subject with little or no information except a native ability to think and reason. The first thing you must do is learn what the terms and symbols mean. As you do this, you are beginning to get experience with the subject. You use these symbols in accordance with the rules or principles set forth, and one day it all begins to make sense to you. In most cases, the complexity comes not from the subject matter or principles, but from the quantity of terms. Terms are made up or selected to describe certain items, situations, locations, changes and whatever else might be observed in the subject or field.

Every subject boils down to observations made by people. Usually these are recorded and compared with other observations taken at different times and places. The principles come from ideas advanced to explain the observations and their relationships logically. As time passes, new observations are recorded requiring new explanations. The terms and labels also change. This evolution is common to all subjects, whether it is medicine or football, and whether it uses Latin or street terms.

Scientific subjects go a step further. The ideas or explanations are used to predict, usually mathematically, future observations, both natural and experimental. In science, ideas are not widely accepted as truth until they have been validated, and the degree of validation determines their degree of truth. Correlation with observable facts and not mere acceptance by others is the key. Truth and open communication are necessary in order for results to be duplicated by others.

This is primarily how science differs from other subjects. As a result, science has been more rigorous and successful, and its achievements are the primary basis of our current civilization.

You might compare the study of any subject with that of learning a new language. There are the terms, symbols and vocabulary on one hand and the principles, rules of usage and syntax on the other. Usually there are relatively few rules and these, normally, align with common sense once you understand them. The terms constitute the bulk of what must be learned.

This is why it is so important that you look up, understand and use the terms in any subject, no matter how much effort it may seem to take at first. Unrecognized vocabulary problems drive students from many subjects. But the students don't realize this; they mistakenly feel that the subject is too complex to grasp or that they are too stupid to master it. You can check this for yourself. Sit down and quiz yourself on the basic terms of any subject. The subjects you know will be those with terms you can define easily and readily. Those you don't know as well will be full of terms that are unclear to you. This is not just a black and white situation. There is a wide range between knowing the subject cold and not knowing it at all, but generally, the vocabulary and experience you have in the subject will indicate your degree of competence and success with it.

There is no reason for you to fear any subject. Talent, natural ability and aptitude are factors, but there is nothing you cannot learn if you put in the requisite effort and persist in your endeavor. Just remember, the complexity lies in the terminology. That is where most difficulties are likely to be found. Following this rule will help you handle most problems with study or new areas of reading.

These principles are true for all forms of material and are particularly useful in technical reading. As you switch from one particular type of material to another, your approach will vary. Let's see how.

Chapter 16

Newspapers, Magazines and Correspondence

Taking a closer look at how to read some specific types of material brings us back to two of our basic principles, "Looking at the Whole — The 3Q's," p. 31 and "Your Approach," p. 33.

Newspapers and most magazines are organized for you. The main idea of a story or an article is put out in a headline or heading. This is often expanded in subheadings. The basic idea, or thrust, is usually put in the first or "lead" paragraph. Ideally, who, what, why, where, when and how are introduced here. Details, facts and the full account follow in the body, and occasionally, there is a final, summarizing paragraph.

A newspaper's front page normally is laid out in the following manner. The main story occupies the upper right column or columns. The next most important story is in the upper left. This way, when you glance across the headlines from left to right, your eyes come to rest on the biggest, most important or most exciting story in the paper, as decided by the editor.

When you read a story's headline or heading, you can begin to see what the whole idea is, what the story is all about, what the parts are and, sometimes, how they are related.

You know how you read the newspaper before this course. You were not a bad reader then and you are not a bad reader now. In fact, you already have all the basic skills necessary for more effective reading. You simply need to reinforce them. Newspaper reading helps and shows how you can use many of these skills.

Most people are fairly proficient at quickly looking over or skimming through a newspaper, especially those who read it on their way to or from work. Do you do this? If not, try it sometime.

A quick look at the story or the headline usually will tell you what the article is about. At this point, most readers go on plugging through the rest of the paper or will stop and read the entire article. This is not wrong, but there is a more efficient method. That is to ask yourself all three questions (The 3 Q's) to determine your approach.

After finding out what the story is about (Q1), stop and ask yourself (Q2), "What do I want from it?" Be sure you answer yourself. Your answer may be entertainment, financial or investment information, data on a candidate, or information concerning the weather. You may be indulging your curiosity. Whatever your answer is, consciously formulating it will make you more aware of what you are doing and trying to accomplish. It will allow you to consciously decide if you want to read the story and how. When your mind is prepared for the material in this manner, it is easier to focus attention upon the subject. This also helps understanding and retention of the material. As you can see, these positive factors support each other.

After determining what you want from the material, but before you go on to read it, ask yourself the third question (Q3), "What do I need from this material?" In many cases, the answer will be nothing. In some cases, you may need to use the information in your job, hobby or school. If such is the case, you will be reading data you want to retain. You cannot approach such material casually.

If you need nothing from the material and want no more from it, then you should pass over it. If you need nothing from it, but want to enjoy it, your reading speed will be determined by the available time. It also will depend on what else you wish to read and the speed at which you comfortably can read it.

You do not have to push yourself through everything. Your time is important, but only you know what is the wisest way to invest it. You know what you are trying to accomplish and what resources you wish to expend in achieving it.

So read the article or story as you wish. If you want to sit back and relax with the story, go right ahead.

When you've finished reading, ask yourself if you actually did get what you needed and wanted. If you didn't, go back and read it again. On this rereading, it may not be necessary to read the whole thing; you should be able to locate and read quickly those parts of which you were uncertain or wish to reconfirm. In either case, make sure you repeat this action as many times as necessary until you succeed in getting what you need.

If you wish to ensure that you can remember what you need, you should stop and think or talk about it for a few seconds. You even may wish to make notes for later use.

Often you will want to read over quickly or skim through the entire paper. You may slow up and read stories of particular interest to you as you go through it all. Another method is to look at the whole paper first and then go back to read those stories that stand out for value or interest. The latter method is the most efficient when your time is limited. This way you can look over everything before deciding how to invest your reading time. This allows you to make the wisest choice based on the fullest information. When more time is available, you need not be so concerned with making the most out of every minute. You may wish to start with your favorite section, be it sports, comics or Dear Abby.

When reading most magazines, you should use the same basic procedures. Technical magazines and materials will be covered in a later chapter.

Your approach also will be affected by the material's content and purpose. One note to keep in mind is that often the title of a magazine or newspaper article is a "leader." It may not be the essential idea of the story; it is there to grab your attention. It may even imply the opposite, or some controversy where there is none. The first job of the article's heading is to attract your attention.

The magazine's or newspaper's editor is trying to make you want to read the article. Perhaps you then will buy the issue or even take out a subscription. Too often what is said is of a lesser importance; what counts is "grabbing" your attention. Getting as many readers as possible is the name of the game because papers and magazines make their living from advertising. Advertising follows readership and pays the bills. These are some of the factors that can lie behind the heading or headline and affect its relationship to the article itself.

The headline's second purpose is to capsulize the article. Often you need to read beyond the heading to determine if you really want to read the material.

All newspapers and magazines follow editorial policies. This means that the publishers decide what to publish and, consequently, what slant or interpretation is given in their publications. In some cases, it is decided by a group of editors. In others, an editorial board is given a framework or a set of guidelines by the owner or owners. But no matter who sets it, there always is some bias or viewpoint.

This usually isn't discussed. In fact, newspapers and magazines often stress that they print the news "straight." The only opinion is supposed to be on the editorial page. But any selecting of what to present necessitates "editing" or choosing what the reader will find out.

In addition, there is the variable of human observation. For example, 10 people view an accident, and afterwards, they are interviewed by a reporter. Each one offers a slightly different version. The overlap and consistencies in their views all go into reconstructing what happened. The absolute truth is impossible to discover because each one saw the accident from a different position. Perhaps one began to see what was happening sooner than the others. Some of them might have had their minds on other things. Many factors make it difficult to reconstruct the complete truth, much less report it.

In some cases, people won't answer reporters' questions. In others, reporters merely accept press releases without investigating further to find out why they were released. Furthermore, reporters don't have a final say on what actually is published, and some of their material may be left out or colored by an editor or rewrite man. Most important of all, there is a deadline to be met and something must be presented and published even if it is not complete, thorough or totally correct. This is true of all news media.

It is not too difficult to discern various viewpoints for yourself, and this is exactly what you should learn to do. Only a portion of a story or news release may be published, or a minor portion may be played up to create controversy. Reporters may bait someone to say something exciting or controversial. Many of their questions are loaded or leading. This is not to say that this is wrong or to advocate censorship. Indeed, the freedom to report the truth is always a continual struggle around the world, and the free flow of information is the only hope there is for personal freedom — it is crucial to a free, democratic society.

What I am pointing out is that individual reporters want to succeed, and they compete for space. In order to be recognized and successful, they need to write news that will be prominent and accepted by their editors. And what is this news? Well, to a large extent, news is controversy, excitement, disaster and information about famous people.

The data is filtered through the viewpoint of the controlling editors. By creating a certain headline or by editing out different parts of a story, entirely different images can emerge.

Here's how to see this for yourself. Buy a copy of every newspaper you can get your hands on for a particular day. Stay with all morning or evening editions wherever possible. If you wish, go to your library, which should have several papers.

Read through the front news section of each. Look at the various headings that run over identical stories. Notice if the same material is presented in the body of the story. Is the information from a news service or the paper's own report-ers? Does this affect the story's treatment? Now do the same for the sports, financial and other sections of the paper.

How much coverage is devoted to international, na-tional, state and local news? If the world or nation is the sub-ject, at what portion is the newspaper looking? How is it viewed? How does this view compare with the ideas expressed in the opinion section? How does this compare with other newspapers? How does it compare with radio and television newscasts?

Do the same with magazines. Do this until you can be-gin to differentiate the various viewpoints.

Another interesting experiment is to do the same thing for material that is 10 or 20 years old. Notice the differences and similarities in today's news.

Try this also on the Internet with "enews" published by the major newspapers, TV networks and other media outlets.

Always use your "Preview" steps when reading on a computer or online. "Look at the Whole;" after a few seconds reading the beginning of the selection, move through it to the end. Then you can ask yourself the 3Q's (page 31).

Why?

Why am I covering all this? Because most of your life you will be exposed to news for your primary source of cur-rent information. You should realize that it is packaged and sold. You are the consumer. It is your interest and attention that is being solicited. You should know how, in what manner and why it is communicated to you. And you should know how to read between the lines.

If you are interested in this area, there is a great deal of information available on journalism in libraries.

But remember, in order to be an effective reader, you must learn to read carefully. Look behind the words. What are the sources? Are they listed? Is this a guess or a projection about the future? How reliable is it? Does it make sense to you? Do you agree? Is it what you think? Why? Why not?

Don't take it all for granted, but instead, look at the actual facts, the trends. Make up your own mind and decide for yourself. This is the best way to read newspapers and magazines. It is how to develop an independent viewpoint. It is also basic to becoming a truly active, discriminating and thoughtful reader.

A large part of being an effective reader is learning exactly what it is you are reading. You must observe the real nature of what's written as well as the content. We'll come back to this concept in the fourth lesson and discuss it further.

Correspondence

Our next type of material is correspondence. This information applies mostly to work-related reading. Business correspondence is an entirely different matter than personal mail, and many executives, secretaries and employees at all levels are faced with a large pile of correspondence every day.

The first rule for effective correspondence handling is to look at the letterhead. What company or organization is it from? The second is to look at the signature. Who sent it to you? What is his position or profession? Then look for the main idea or gist of the communication. Usually this is in the middle paragraph.

From this point, there are two ways to go, depending on the amount of correspondence, what your job duties are and how much time you have. If time permits, handle the matter immediately. Then you have it out of your way and it's another piece of your work accomplished.

Sometimes though, the volume of correspondence, available time, required job duties or a combination of these factors, do not permit this immediate handling. In this case, go through each piece quickly. It should take only a few seconds for each one. Then place each piece into one of two piles.

The first pile consists of those items you can dispatch quickly. They may take a short reply, or you already know how to handle them.

The second pile contains more difficult items that cannot be handled immediately. These may take research, checking with someone else, or other necessary steps before handling. They will take more time and work.

Handling the first pile is usually your priority after sorting all your correspondence. This way you are handling those items that can be done right away and getting much of your work done. Then turn to the second pile and begin to handle it.

Use these same basic approaches for email. Who sent it? Look at the subject line; if that's not enough information, look through the email quickly. What is the gist of it? If necessary, look through to the end. Ask yourself the 3Q's (page 31), then decide what to do with the email.

There often are exceptions, other duties and priorities you need to attend to, and you may evolve your own system. If you do, the most important guidelines are to organize your duties and time as well as your reading approach. This will give you the greatest overall savings in time and effort.

Using the note-taking system introduced in the study chapter may also be helpful as well as using the information in the technical reading chapter.

Chapter 17

Pleasure Reading

Reading for pleasure is one of life's greatest joys. You should decide how you wish to read something for your own pleasure and read it that way. If you just want to sit back and relax, then by all means do so. Lose yourself, live the story and take as long as you like.

Are you wondering what kind of advice this is to be coming from a "speedreading" manual? Does it seem strange? Well, it shouldn't.

The purpose of Power Reading is to give you more control over your life and time. The idea is not for you to just whiz through everything. The idea is for you to be able to face and handle the mountain of material you need to read in order to survive well and succeed in life. At the same time, you want to be able to enjoy yourself. Speed works best when it's used as one tool in your toolbox of reading skills. Use it as a buzz saw to cut through to what you need and want. You can slow it down or speed it up and feel free to shut it off when you desire.

One of the advantages of being an effective reader is that the time you save on the things you need to read may be used for anything you wish. Almost everyone has things he or she would really like to read, and sitting down with a book is one of life's greatest pleasures.

So enjoy yourself. As you do, you will find you are naturally reading faster even when you read for pleasure.

If you are reading poetry, feel free to read aloud. That's the way it's written and meant to be read. Act out a play if you wish. Stop and contemplate a great thought. There are no rules or limits to reading for pleasure.

Personally, I find that the better the book, the longer I want it to last. There is no need to hurry when "living" the story or adventure, and the more I wish to savor it, the slower I go.

Here is another point when reading non-fiction books. Say you have one on pollution, history or politics, but the whole book isn't as interesting as a particular chapter. Then start with that chapter after you have previewed the entire book. Beginning with the material you are interested in will usually lead to exploring the rest of the author's ideas. This can be done at whatever speed you wish.

Religious reading is in a category by itself. You may wish to read aloud or silently, and in most cases, you will want to read at a speaking pace. Usually this is not the place for speed, but for careful study, contemplation, recitation and prayer. You should follow your own feelings and faith in your religious reading.

There is one idea that is workable in every type of material. When you read something that you like, you have found a new friend — the author. Often, this friend has written other works which you are also likely to enjoy. This is as true in Shakespeare's classics as in Agatha Christie's mysteries. When you find such friends, your enjoyment will be increased as you get to know them even better.

There are no set, unbreakable rules for getting information or pleasure from a book or author. The important standard of measurement is your understanding and enjoyment. You make the rules and please yourself!

Chapter 18

Reading and Drilling

Up to now we have concerned ourselves primarily with reading and improving comprehension. We've been working on understanding what is being read and going back over the material when there is any doubt about comprehension.

In this lesson, we began working on speed and then started examining perception and how reading works. Also, we discussed what slows you down and how you can overcome those habits.

You know that using a regulator will increase your reading rate. Even as you take in and understand individual words and the overall meaning, you will speed up. Now we are going to emphasize this process with practicing or drilling.

Practicing, or drilling, is entirely different than reading. You should get all the comprehension you desire when you read. When you practice or drill for speed, however, the emphasis is different. You will get some comprehension, but that is not your primary purpose when you practice or drill. The purpose of drilling is to help you get the idea and feel for what it is like to read even faster. If you never go at a faster pace than walking, how can you learn to run? You need to push yourself to practice in order to get faster, stronger and better. This is true no matter what you attempt.

If you never try to read faster or at high speeds, you obviously won't achieve them. You need to experience seeing the words go past at a faster rate before you can begin to read them. This can be done for you by a machine, or you can actively pursue it yourself. Some effort is necessary, and the more you work at it, the more you will achieve.

You already have some experience with this. It's what you've been doing every day for 5 minutes during the past week. Speed was the purpose of having you reread the 10 minutes worth of material in 5 minutes. A secondary purpose was to help with comprehension, which increases when you go back over the material. This happens when you see what you read, what else was there and what you forgot or missed. But this extra comprehension was a bonus; speed was the goal. You will always get some comprehension when you practice for speed, but you should not let it slow you down while drilling.

Reading Versus Drilling

Do not get confused here. You should not sacrifice comprehension when you read. Absolutely not. But when you drill, you should push for speed. The difference is reading versus drilling.

As we have seen, if you are not comprehending what you want or need, you are not reading by our definition. We're using a strict, narrow definition that puts a great deal of responsibility on you, the reader. Merely seeing the words is not enough, because you must understand what you are reading and be satisfied that you are doing so. You must get what you want and need from the material when you read it.

When you practice, however, you are pushing primarily for speed. So do not worry about comprehension when you are trying to find out what it is like to read much faster than you usually do. This has to begin with your looking at more words in a given period of time. During the daily 5-minute practice period last week, you "practiced" approximately twice as fast as you read and looked at twice as many words in the same time.

Then it was all right if you didn't cover all the material in 5 minutes. But this week we're working on speed, and it matters. This week I want you to make sure you cover in 5 minutes all the material you read in 10 minutes. This still can be done using work, school or pleasure material. You can read for 10 minutes at one time or spread it out. It is more beneficial, however, to do the 10-minute reading in a single sitting. If necessary, you can use your lunch hour or some time after work or school, but you definitely should set aside 15 minutes daily.

Remember, when you go over the material the second time in 5 minutes, you are practicing, not reading. Your chief concern is to complete the drill. Pace yourself. Regulate your speed. Don't spend 4 minutes on the first third of the material and then try to cover the remaining two-thirds in the last minute.

Go quickly where you can follow the thought easily and leave yourself more time in difficult areas. Spend the most time on the main points and ideas, but get through it all in the allotted 5 minutes. This is the most important objective of this exercise: to get through all the material in 5 minutes. This will make you practice faster than you can read.

In addition to reading for 10 minutes and practicing for speed over the same material in 5 minutes, there will be one more task. That is to look quickly over, or preview, the 10-minute selection of material before you read it. You will have to estimate how many pages you will be able to read in the 10-minute period. This preview should take from 30 seconds to a minute, but no more.

You are not trying to "read" during the preview. Your only purpose is to look over the material. How long is it? Are there pictures or graphs? What is it about? Don't let yourself get hung up and don't get bogged down. Decide what you need and want and keep in mind that you are just trying to familiarize yourself with the material. To read, preview or drill faster, just cover less of the line with your regulator and force your eyes to keep up.

You need to do this 10-minute reading and 5-minute drilling at least once a day this week to get the minimum results promised from this course. If you wish to increase your gains, then drill more than once a day. The more you drill, the more you will improve. But don't overdo it or try to do it all at once.

It is better to repeat one drill at different times. Rest a few minutes, walk around or do a different type of work or activity between complete drill cycles. Doing one cycle of read 10, practice 5 right after the other will not lead to the maximum gain. You will achieve better results by spacing the exercise periods throughout the day, and it will take less effort.

So by all means, practice all you wish, but space out the sessions. Don't try to rush yourself, because you won't progress nearly as well as when you take a little more time to groove in these new skills. And when you read, comprehend.

Of course, it is still important that you use a regulator on everything you read and not just when you drill.

Before you leave this lesson, try this drill once in your practice material. Really push for speed and cover all the material.

Next week we'll discuss different approaches for various types of materials. I'll see you then.

Chapter 19

2nd Week's Exercises

1. Set aside at least 15 minutes to read each day.
2. Quickly look over what you can read in 10 minutes. Try to do this in 30 seconds, but take no more than one minute.
3. Read for 10 minutes for full comprehension.
4. Cover this material again in 5 minutes. Be sure you cover it all in the allotted time. Remember, this is practice for speed, not comprehension.
5. Fill in your daily log.
6. Use your regulator on everything you read.

Supplemental Reading

This second week I recommend that you read *A History of Reading* by Alberto Manguel, Penguin Books, New York, 1997. It will take you on the fascinating journey of reading's history from the ancient Sumerians up to modern times.

Log 2nd Week

8th Day:
Today I read_____
                         (name of book or type of material)

for_____
                         (length of time)

9th Day:
    Today I read_____

      for_____

10th Day:
    Today I read_____

      for_____

11th Day:
    Today I read_____

      for_____

12th Day:
    Today I read_____

      for_____

13th Day:
    Today I read_____

      for_____

14th Day:
    Today I read_____

      for_____

3rd WEEK – LESSON III

Thinking leads men to knowledge. One may see and hear and read and learn as much as he pleases; he will never know any of it except that which he has thought over, that which by thinking he has made the property of his mind...

Hohann Heinrich Pestalozzi

Chapter 20

Mid-Course Exam

I hope you have had another good week and have done a lot of reading. We're at the halfway point now, but still have a lot more to cover in the course.

This week we are going to look at reading technical material, study and test taking.

Speaking of tests, we are ready to take the mid-course evaluation and see how you've progressed so far. You need to use your original material, the same book as in Lesson I. Start from where you ended the first test and repeat the reading exam exactly as given in Lesson I. Read for 10 minutes and then mark your ending spot.

10-Minute Reading Exam

Very good. Did you mark your ending point? Now we'll repeat the comprehension evaluation.

Summarize as fully as possible what you've just read in the last 10 minutes. Do this on the Mid-Course Reading Summary.

Mid-Course Reading Summary

Date:_____

Book Title:_____

Page began reading:_____

Page ended reading:_____

Summary:_____

_____

_____

_____

_____

_____

_____

Now let's compute your present speed.

Just multiply the average number of words per page (Answer 4 from Lesson I) by the number of pages you read this time. This will give the total number of words you just read. Since you read for 10 minutes, divide this figure by 10 and you'll have your speed in wpm:

_____ words per page (Answer 4 in Lesson I, page 9)

X_____ pages read in final 10-minute reading

=_____ total number of words read in 10 minutes

Now divide by 10:

$$\frac{\text{(total words read)}}{10} = \underline{\hspace{2cm}} \text{ (your speed in wpm.)}$$

Now write down both your initial speed and the date and your mid-term speed and today's date.

Wpm initial speed_____on _____
                                                                      (date)

Wpm mid-term speed_____ on _____
                                                                    (date)

How do they compare?

You can see your relative increase in percentage by doing the following:
Divide the difference in these rates by your initial speed and multiply by 100.

EXAMPLE: initial wpm = 264
                    mid-term wpm = 396

mid-term wpm - initial wpm = difference

396 (mid-term wpm) – 264 (initial wpm) = 132 (difference)

$$\frac{132 \text{ (difference)}}{264 \text{ (initial wpm)}} \times 100 = 50\% \text{ increase.}$$

Now calculate your results:

_____mid-term wpm – _____initial wpm = _____ (difference)

$$\frac{\text{(difference)}}{\text{(initial wpm)}} \times 100 = \underline{\hspace{2cm}} \% \text{ increase.}$$

This is how much faster you are reading at this point.

What about your comprehension? Look over your mid-term summary once again and answer the following questions:

1. Did you feel you understood what the author said?
    Yes_____No_____
2. Do you feel you got the main ideas?
    Yes_____No_____
3. Do you feel you got the basic facts?
    Yes_____No_____

Now quickly reread the material to check yourself.

Quickly Reread the Test Material to Check Your Comprehension

Now look at your summary again and then answer the following questions:

1. Did you understand it as well as you thought earlier?
    Yes_____No_____

2. Did you understand the main idea/ideas correctly?
    Yes_____No_____

3. Did you get the basic facts?
    Yes_____No_____

4. Did you get enough from your first reading to satisfy you as you look back now?
    Yes_____No_____

5. How much do you feel you correctly understood?
   All_____ Most _____Enough_____Not enough_____
   Little_____

6. Do you feel you understood it when you read it, but couldn't remember as much when you went to summarize it?
   Yes_____No_____

7. Are you satisfied with your present level of comprehension?
   Yes_____No_____

8. Would you like to improve your comprehension?
   Yes_____No_____

9. Do you feel you need to work most on:
   Comprehension_____Speed_____or both_____

Record your results here:

My current reading speed is_____wpm.

I am reading_____% faster than when I began.

I am achieving my goal satisfactorily because:_____

_____

_____

_____

_____

I am not achieving my results satisfactorily. I believe the reason is:_____

_____

_____

_____

I intend to change this situation by: _____

_____

_____

_____

If you are progressing satisfactorily, excellent; just continue the course and have fun. If you are not progressing satisfactorily, then consult the appropriate chapter that discusses your difficulty. See if you can pinpoint the source of your questions and look for the answer in the chapter that is applicable; also you can consult the index. Most problems resolve easily when the techniques necessary to handle them are located and applied.

The majority of students are reading about half again faster by now. How are you doing? Are you close to this level? Are you above or below it? Don't worry if you are below it a little. Just push yourself a bit more if you wish to make your goals. But if you are above this level, don't slack off now. Keep on pushing yourself. We're only halfway there.

If you've wondered what is the best method for reading technical and study materials, this is the lesson that will answer your questions.

Chapter 21

Technical Reading

Reading technical material is a further use of the skills you have been developing. There are many factors that come into play here. Your background, or how much you already know about what you are studying, is one of the most important.

If you are already familiar with the vocabulary and terminology, it will be possible to read faster than when it is new and strange to you.

Technical material is a special category of communication. It consists of highly concentrated facts and symbols in a very organized, tightly reasoned presentation.

Quickly preview such material first. Read the introduction and conclusion and briefly glance at the body of the material to see what it's about. Once again, you can read the first or last sentences in paragraphs as these introduce and summarize the main ideas presented. You can read introductory and concluding sections. In this way, you can determine what it contains and what conclusions the author draws. But in order to fully understand all the details and procedures, you must go back and read carefully. As you read, you are recreating the experiment or research in your mind and looking at its results. If you are already familiar with the type of experience the author is recounting, it will be fairly easy for you to read and comprehend.

If you are entering a particular subject for the first time, it can be more difficult. You may need to consult a specialized dictionary, other reference works or earlier background material. At times, you may want to repeat the experiment. There are no magical quick steps for absorbing technical knowledge; you must work your way through it. It will take as long as it takes you to understand the terms and to think your way through them.

You can get the overall idea quickly and easily, but an exact reconstruction in your mind of what the author is saying will take more effort and concentration. Sometimes, however, this is not necessary. You may only want to find out who is doing what and how and what conclusions are being drawn. Often, this can be done with a quick preview or reading.

Taking notes as you read is an excellent habit to cultivate. It is covered more fully in the next section on study. A consolidation of these notes onto 3x5 or 4x6 cards is a handy method of establishing your own "permanent" cross-reference, memory file system. Copying or cutting out articles and storing them in folders and file cabinets can also be useful. However, it has the disadvantage of becoming bulky very quickly and storage can be troublesome.

Another note-taking method is to use 8.5x11 inch or legal size note pads. Be sure to leave room in the margins to add more notes later on.

Computer documents and Internet articles can be stored in file folders you name for the subjects they contain. Often it is a good idea to put the year as part of the name of the folder that contains all of the subject matter documents or articles stored in that year. It is extremely important to take a few extra moments and clearly label and date the file or article so you can easily find it later. One of the biggest mistakes people make is to put a short generic label on a file. This can waste hours or make the information unfindable months or years later. For example, "technical reading methods - Power Reading_2002" versus a generic "techread." In file naming, the use of spaces, dashes, commas, underlines or "underscores" and dating (which may include month-day-year) is up to each individual.

The two most important factors are to know what the information is and where to find it. The journals and other publications are available in libraries or online, but what you must know is which article you need. Making your own card file and/or computerized system is one of the best methods of keeping this information for yourself.

Technical information comes in many formats. You can easily see what they are as you do your own research and investigations. Usually directions and instructions are included in journals and reference works. Going to the library or onto the Internet and investigating for yourself is the best way to familiarize yourself with available information and its presentation.

Technical reading utilizes the same three basics we have used throughout this book: "Looking at the Whole or Preview," "Your Approach" and "Regulating Speed." "Your Approach" differs in the care you give to technical material. You will read it a number of times. This is a multiple reading approach. It bridges over into the field of learning and study handled in the next chapter; everything covered there is applicable to technical reading.

The main difference that is you are usually less familiar with study material, so the reading process is more exacting. Most students are not sure of what they need from the material because they lack experience with the subject. Technical readers, on the other hand, usually have a clearer conception of what they are reading and why. They are keeping abreast and adding to their store of information, not learning and trying to organize it for the first time. Thus, it is easier for them to comprehend and judge when they have read enough.

The basic procedure for technical reading is to follow the path established by previewing, finding out what the material is about and determining what you want or need from it. Then reread the material as thoroughly as necessary. Finally, a quick review is helpful to remember the information for later use, and written notes will give you a permanent record. Later review will keep it fresh in your mind.

We will see this procedure again in even more detail in the next chapter on study.

Chapter 22

Study

Studying is what a student does in order to learn. It is the directed, purposeful application of one's mind to understand and use a subject. Study can take place under the guidance of an instructor or on one's own. In either case, the actual process of study is the same.

There is a difference for many students when it comes to studying a subject they actually will be using in life versus one they are only trying to memorize for a test. The basic procedures for studying are the same, but the purposes are entirely different. One day your life may depend on knowing and remembering what you once studied; this happens daily in driving a car. On the other hand, you may need to take a certain history course, but have little desire to do more than get a good grade. If so, it is likely you are not motivated to learn and retain the information permanently, and usually you won't. Make sure you don't do this when you study something you need to use in life.

While reading encompasses 70 – 80% of most college work, there is far more to the process of study. One of the biggest myths among students is that study just consists of reading assigned pages and reviewing them before an exam. Unfortunately, this "once over" reading method is only a part of the study process and does not work well by itself.

Research has shown that more effective learning comes from repetition rather than from a single application. Seeing or reading something once does not ensure that you will learn it. The more times you go over it, the better you will learn it.

Generally, learning is accelerated in an environment that includes breaks rather than uninterrupted, prolonged sessions. Neither 6 hours nor 5 minutes is the best length for your study sessions. Take a break every hour or so; do something different before coming back. Some people find 20 to 40 minutes of concentrated study followed by a 5 to 10-minute break and then a 2 to 10-minute review and note-taking period to be most effective before proceeding on to new material.

You will retain what you have learned much longer by studying it over again. Study until you get it and then a bit more. This "overlearning" gives you better retention. No matter how well you learn, you will begin to forget some of it immediately. Without additional review, you can forget 80 – 90% or more of what you have learned within 24 hours. With periodic review, you can remember it indefinitely. So sitting down and reading something once is not the best method for study. It is only part of the overall study process.

Study begins with establishing your purpose clearly in your mind. This should be done each time you study.

Why are you studying this material? Is it for a test? Is it background research? Is it something you will have to do and use in your life or work? How soon do you need to use this information? These questions, and more, are important.

There is one basic difference between study and all other types of reading. When you study, you are usually responsible to someone or something other than yourself for the information. It may be an instructor, an employer, nature or the stock market, but you need to get and remember not only what you want, but also what is required. And what you need is not determined by you alone, but by the purpose for which you are studying.

Two factors are crucial: first, you must understand the information correctly and fully, and secondly, you must be able to remember and use it when you need it. These are two separate processes. Understanding and remembering are not the same thing, although they are interdependent.

Long-Term Memory

As we learned earlier, it takes only about 1/4th of a second to fixate and register information on your retina. It takes another 1/4th of a second to process it into your short-term memory so that you can see it. Now, here is a key point: it takes at least 5 seconds of concentration on any piece of information to store it in your long-term memory so that you can have good recall and use of it later. This is why, after looking up a word in the dictionary, you need to use it in sentences in order to remember it. Similarly, reciting things and writing notes will help you remember data for an exam or later use. Active use promotes remembering. Passive observation promotes forgetting. Our minds selectively filter out what we don't use in order to save room for what we need for future use. You learn and remember by observation and use of information.

It is unrealistic to expect to glance at a page and later to remember it verbatim. What you can do, though, is to learn and use the most effective methods for study. These will increase your ability to retain and use the necessary information far more than wishing you had a photographic memory.

Motivation

Motivation usually is discussed as a prime factor and often a problem in teaching and learning. Studies have shown that when a student is interested in something, he learns it faster and better. Much has been written about allowing students more freedom and latitude to pursue their interests and learn at their own rates. But it is difficult, if not impossible, in the current mass educational system. It is practiced in a few, mostly private schools, but takes more time, materials, expense and guidance than are presently available in most public schools.

This does not mean that a student should not or cannot pursue his or her own interests. In fact, the more a student relates his interests to what he needs to study, the more successful he can be.

You can control this because it is an individual factor. If a subject seems uninteresting, you can make it interesting; find out more about it. Get some books on it and find out how it relates to the world. How did it come about? Who is interested in it and why? How does it or how can it affect your life? What is interesting about it? Search for the answers.

Not everyone is a student, but at some point, everyone becomes interested in a field or topic. This is when learning is most pleasurable because you can follow the path of your own interest. This, of course, can be done in school, night school, college, correspondence school, part-time, or even on your own. Education for the mind is like physical activity for the body. Exercise it and you expand your mental abilities just as, for example, fixing cars or participating in athletics can both lead you to physics in order to improve yourself in either field.

While learning, the multiple skills of reading and comprehension come into play. Understanding and following the main and subordinate ideas, paying attention to details, understanding the symbols and their significance, predicting outcomes and conclusions and aligning information are the mental skills used in the learning process. These are most enjoyable when done for your own purposes. Then, as you go along and begin to grasp the whole and the parts, their labels and names, interactions and relationships, it is fun because you are accomplishing what you want to do. You begin to think with and use the concepts. You enjoy the fun of learning and the pleasure of achieving your own goals.

If you are interested in something, it is usually meaningful to you. They go hand in hand. With them for motivation, the mind finds it much easier to learn and recall the data. Parts seem to fit together more easily and logically in a discernible fashion. These logical units, or wholes, are easier to grasp and relate to than individual or isolated facts. This is why it is better to study whole ideas or sections rather than to read a certain number of pages during a study session.

If you feel you are studying something uninteresting, then make it easier on yourself. Find out more about it. Time spent on developing and cultivating an interest in the subject will pay off in the long run. Do some extra research and find out how and why you should be interested in the subject. How does this subject affect your life? How is it being used in the world? What is its history? How has it affected other people? No subject is totally uninteresting or unrelated to your personal life.

Lectures

Sometimes students complain about a teacher's lectures. This is understandable when the teacher is merely rehashing or, worse yet, reading from the textbook. The classroom lecture system is an institution that dates back to the medieval ages and earlier times when books were rare and generally unavailable.

A scholar or teacher would read to the class from the book because there were no copies available for the students to read themselves. The few manuscripts they had were too fragile and valuable to let everyone read and handle them. When the book was not available, the teacher would read from his own notes, perhaps taken when he was a student. Teachers lecturing and reading to their students was the most practical method of communicating information before the printing press. To do this when students have their own books and have already read the material is a waste of time. It also encourages students not to bother reading the material themselves.

On the other hand, it might be that the student could not follow the lecture because he neglected to read the previously assigned material. Or there might be words used in the lecture that were not clearly understood by the student. The remedy is taking notes and looking up the words later. It is also good to check with others in the class from time to time to ensure the correctness and completeness of your notes and comprehension.

Wider reading in the subject will also increase understanding of what is being covered in class and the required texts. It also will help build interest in the subject. And this is one of the keys to successful study.

Preparation is important. Naturally, you should do your studying where you won't be interrupted or distracted. The lighting should be good, you shouldn't be hungry and you should have all the necessary supplies on hand. These are all prerequisites to study.

Time Management

Another prerequisite is time management. Many students need to set and maintain a fairly rigid study schedule, and all students need to keep exact track of their semester, testing and projects, as well as their weekly schedule. A large calendar is a necessity for this task.

Almost all problems with study start with a lack of effective time management. If you are having trouble with your time management, list your activities and assign priorities to them. Then take your high priority items and build a weekly schedule around them and stick to it. When you have everything under control, you can begin to relax a little after your grades are where you want them. By handling your time effectively, you will be more relaxed and find it easier to concentrate when you study.

Start Slowly, Then Speed Up

As you begin to study, work yourself into it. Don't try to do it all at once. Often starting with a preview of what you are studying, then slowly, carefully getting into the material will soon lead you to a more rapid, comfortable pace. Skipping over or missing things at the beginning of your study session can start you off on a frustrating waste of your time and energy. Just as you want to get a firm grounding in any subject, you want to do the same with any study period.

The 3 Keys

Interest, attention and repetition are the 3 keys to effective study and retention of information.

Effective study consists of a multiple reading process (covering the material 3 or more times), active thinking, questioning, innovative note-taking, reflection and periodic review. As you already know from your daily exercises, when you read something over a second time, you get more from it. This is true no matter what the speed, because repetition improves comprehension.

At first, some students resist this approach because they feel they do not have the time to read through study material several times. They might as well say they don't have time to study, because, as we have seen, you usually need to go over something several times to really learn it. However, you don't have to go over it the same way each time.

When you study, you will read differently each time you cover the material. Your first time through the material should be very quick. This is a fast preview which serves to show you what the material is about, how long it is, how it's laid out and what you are going to be covering.

Always try to select a logical unit, section or subsection to study. Study by ideas, not by the clock. Try to grasp and comprehend complete thoughts; don't just study by the hour. Studying logical units is the most effective approach and should be used whenever possible.

Preview — Look at the Whole

Preview your study section quickly; read the introduction and summary if these are included. Studying isn't like reading a mystery; you want every bit of help available no matter if it's at the beginning or at the end of the material.

In your preview step, look over the charts, graphs and pictures. Remember, you can read the first or last sentences in paragraphs as these introduce and summarize the main ideas presented. You can read introductory and concluding sections. You will get a good idea of what's being covered and will prepare yourself for what you are about to read. Then, after previewing, ask yourself questions about what you're going to study. See how much you know first, then read to add to it.

Study Reading

Now comes your second time through the material. Read through the section carefully and thoroughly. Make sure you understand what you are reading as you read it. At this point in your studying you are reading for full comprehension. Don't go past anything without understanding it. Look up those words; look at a map and find out where that place is located.

Make a dot (.) or check (✔) in the margin to signify importance. Most students waste too much time and effort underlining in pen, pencil or marking pen. Using a ruler to make straight lines is more time-consuming. Looking back later, students usually see that they've underlined far too much, missed a great deal of what's really important and generally made a messy tangle of lines in the textbook. Of course, they don't realize this until later when they look back at their textbook with the fuller understanding that comes with the second and third readings. The time spent concentrating on underlining often could be spent better concentrating on learning.

Underlining

This doesn't mean underlining or marking a textbook is bad. The purpose of underlining is to point out the important items. It's a symbol that says: "Don't miss this!" But a dot or check mark in the margin can do the same, and you can put one there each time you read the material. This way the most important items will have several dots or checks next to them. Those with only one mark are ideas that you thought were important at first, but later realized that they weren't. For later review, your mark will show not only what is important, but also how important it is in comparison with the rest of the data. So study-read with a pencil as your regulator and put a dot in the margin to signify importance.

You can see how the important information stands out. It's not too hard to see which method will be more effective for later review and study. If you still wish to underline key words,

Checks

Dots

Checks, Dots and Underlines

which is fine, I suggest you do it on your review step when you understand and can evaluate the information more fully.

Review

After this careful study reading, quickly review or look through the section again to see how it all fits together. Add anything you've missed to what you already have and be sure that you've understood the material correctly and completely. See the overall idea and notice how each subordinate item fits into the picture. Organize it for yourself. Use the information to make it yours.

This is where your memory comes into play. Studies have shown that the best way to remember is to understand clearly and to relate the information to what you already know. You want to see it in a logical, orderly pattern. The more connections you can make, the better you will remember it. Visualizing it in some fashion is an excellent tool. Trying to picture how it fits together is your goal when you review the material.

This review will be your third time over the material. Usually it is a quick step. The first reading was the preview step; it too should be fast. The second time over the material was your thorough study reading. This is a slow, complete reading.

Then the third reading is a quick review. It is when you pull it all together, double check your understanding and really begin to work on actively using and remembering the material.

Going over the material several times like this is what helps you understand it best. For one thing, you do not feel pressured to get it all the first time and you will add to your understanding with subsequent rereadings. You can concentrate on understanding it fully at first, then work on remembering it for later. This organization can free you from the frustration that comes from trying to do too much at once.

Use It

At the end of each reading, try to use the information. This is how to get it into your long-term memory for later use. Ask yourself questions and answer them. Write outlines, notes, summaries or fill out note cards. Talk about it with someone else. Try to explain it and answer questions so you will see what you don't know. Think about how this information fits in with what else you know and have studied.

Again, the best way to understand and retain something is to use it or do something with it. If you can't, you don't really know it and need to go back to it. Do the problems and exercises.

This is the best way I know to study mathematics and other highly specific and technical languages. Reading the formulas is just the start. You need to work the problems thoroughly to grasp and be able to use the concepts in practice. This is how you get them into your mind for later use. If you can't do the problems, you need to go back and see what step you missed. If necessary, get help. Don't wait or put it off.

Answer the questions given or make up your own. Do both. Using the information in some fashion will give you a check on your understanding and ensure that you know it. Often the best way to truly learn something is to explain or teach it to someone else. You will quickly begin to spot your confusions and see what else you need to study.

You should spend at least 25% of your total study time actually using the information in some way if you want to keep it fresh in your memory. This can go as high as 50%, or more if necessary. After finishing your study, take a quick look at your notes after a short break and again the following day. Two to 10 minutes should suffice for these reviews.

One classic experiment with retention compared students who only passively read and reread material with those who spent varying amounts of time actively using and reciting it. Those in the group who spent the most time using and reciting the material were able to recall three times as much as those who only passively read the material. This step of actively using the information is your key to retention and accurate recall.

Periodic Review

The mind has evolved to selectively forget what is unnecessary in order to make room for the continual inflow of new information. That which is necessary to analyze and make decisions about new events is retained. Everything may be stored away, but only what you use in your daily life and work is readily available. The rule here is "use it or lose it." It is a fundamental principle that is applicable to the rest of your life as well as to study. Applying it works.

Anything you have studied will come back to you more easily later when you study it again. This is similar to swimming or bicycle riding. You never forget these skills entirely. "Brushing up" or relearning them is much easier and faster than learning them for the first time. Whatever you don't use, your mind stores away to make room for new information that you will use. So if you want to remember something, you must use it.

A quick look at your study notes from 10 minutes to an hour after you have completed studying them and another look the next day will reinforce your retention even further. Everything you see, experience, study and learn competes for your available memory capacity. The new tends to push out the old, and conversely, what you already have learned affects what you currently are learning. What you learn later also will have an effect. You must use any information to keep it from being pushed out of your consciously accessible memory.

Therefore, the more you reinforce your memory on each subject you study through understanding, association and review, the better off you will be.

This is another reason why you should try to relate what you are learning to everything else possible. Memory tricks and systems have been known and studied for thousands of years, but they have never replaced straightforward, logical study. The more logical connections and relationships you can draw, the more firmly the information is lodged in your memory, and the more it will help your retention of the material for later use. The more you use it, the less likely you are to lose it.

After you have completed these steps, you will need to review periodically. To review, look over your notes, outlines and margin marks thoroughly. Do this as often as necessary; at least every few days or weeks. Recite aloud. Review with one or two other people and quiz yourselves. Once again you must use the information to keep it fresh and usable. Otherwise, it will fade away. This is what happens with any subject or foreign language you don't use. Once again, use it or lose it.

5 Steps

Here are the 5 steps for effective study:

1. Preview — Quickly look over the material. Find out what it is about, how it is organized and what you want from it. Note graphs, pictures and charts. Read the introduction and summary. Question yourself or start your notes before you read it.

2. Read thoroughly — Emphasize full understanding of what you are reading, look up and define any words or terms of which you are unsure and realize that you do not need to remember everything from only this step. Concentrate on reading and understanding thoroughly. You can make notes before your review if you wish, as well as after.

3. Review — Quickly reread the material for the third time. Look for the organization and interrelationships, visualize the patterns and material and put it all into a coherent whole.

4. Use the information — Talk about it, take notes, outline, summarize, draw it, think about it, and connect it with what else you know. This should be at least 25% of your budgeted study time. Remember, use it or lose it.

5. Review periodically — Go back over what you have studied, as often as necessary. Every few days or weeks is sufficient.

These instructions are a guide. You do not have to follow them exactly, but you should read the material at least three times. Use it for 1/4 or more of your study time and periodically review it.

Trying to do all your studying the night before an exam is better than not studying at all, but it is neither advisable nor very effective. Unfortunately, it is the favorite method of many students, and usually their grades suffer because of it. As easy as it may seem at first, you are better off not getting into this habit. In the long run, it doesn't pay.

Test Taking

Here are some general tips you may find helpful when taking tests. Relax as much as possible just before and during the test. Worrying yourself into a frazzle will do you no good and uses up energy that could be better expended on concentration.

When you get the test, preview it quickly. Note how long it is, how many questions there are and of what types. Allocate a time limit for each section and leave yourself some time for review. Skip any particularly hard questions and come back to them after you have answered the ones you do know. This will help maximize your score.

Read each question accurately and review it if necessary before answering it. Silly mistakes are often the most costly, and they can be easily avoided. If you need to guess, try to eliminate any wrong answers you can spot. This will increase your chances of getting the right answer. Usually your first guess is your best bet. This is not a guarantee, but it is a good general rule.

Watch out for trick questions, absolutes (always, never, etc.) and items designed to throw you off. Use your common sense and, most importantly, when a test is over, let it go. Don't worry about it. If you don't do well, it's not the end of the world. Usually you can do more work for extra credit, perhaps take a retest, or talk to the teacher and try to make up for your "failure." No situation is hopeless unless you give up. Teachers want to teach and give you a chance to learn. This is not an invitation to goof off, but it is an encouragement to try harder if, at first, you don't succeed.

While you do not have to use the techniques given here for study, you will discover that your study efficiency will improve markedly once they are practiced and become second nature to you. At first, they may seem to take more time and effort, but they will work and save you time if you use them. In addition, your grades may well improve. Go over them carefully, try them, practice them and then use them.

When reading technical material, use this same approach. Naturally you will want to shorten it for some material. You may find it most effective to use a filing system such as 3x5 cards to keep and cross reference data for future use.

Some note-taking system is essential for supplementing your long-term memory and giving you permanent reference to the information. Taking notes causes you to physically use another section of your brain, creating more neural interconnections and resulting in better memory. The next chapter will show several methods of taking notes.

Chapter 23

Note-Taking

Taking notes is the process of taking in, condensing and writing down information in some organized fashion so that you can use it later. You need to write down enough to clearly understand and remember it later. You should avoid recording too much information, however. Your periodic reviews will help you learn how much you need to record.

An Example of the Outline Form of Taking Notes

I.   STUDY (Chapter Title or Main Idea)
    A. PREVIEW (Sub-Idea)
        1. LOOK OVER WHOLE (Data-Facts-Specifics)
           a. determine main idea
           b. determine what is needed
           c. determine what is wanted
    B. READ CAREFULLY
II.   Etc.
    A. Etc.
        1. Etc.
           a. etc.
           b. etc.
           c. etc.

It is set and fairly inflexible, yet very practical and workable.

There are other methods that serve the same function, but have a more flexible form. They take the same information and display it differently. Whereas most outline forms follow a chronological organization, the flexible ones may follow a chronological or informational (i.e. main idea, subordinate idea, supporting data, etc.) approach.

Here are some examples:

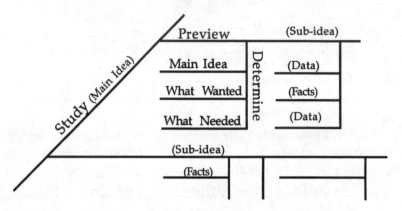

EXAMPLES OF VISUAL DISPLAY NOTE-TAKING:

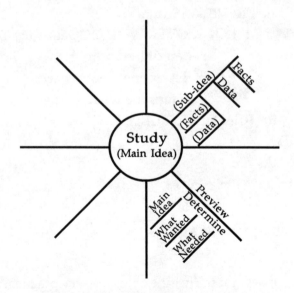

These have the advantage of holding more information in a form that easily can be visualized on a single page.

Outlines are restricted to a linear format, but the more flexible forms can take any format.

If you read a great deal of technical material, then you should take notes on 3x5 or 4x6 cards for later reference. Try all these formats for your note-taking before making a final decision about which method is best for you.

FLOW CHARTS ARE ANOTHER APPROACH TO NOTE -TAKING

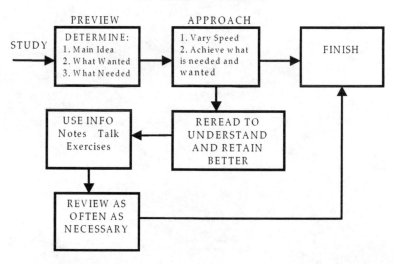

You need to write down enough so it will be easy to understand at some later date, so don't skimp now and end up having to redo the whole process later. On the other hand, condense the information as much as possible. Be concise as well as clear.

Subject titles at the top of cards are especially helpful for cross-referencing and integrating information.

Remember, this is your "permanent" memory. The information you record now can help you months or years after it has been "pushed" out of your conscious memory by new information and events. The benefits from note-taking are twofold. As you use the material, you are building and working for the future while you help yourself to understand more fully in the present.

Another excellent use for note cards is in studying vocabulary, our next subject.

Chapter 24

Vocabulary

The more difficult or technical the material, the more careful and thorough you will have to be with its terms, words and symbols. This new vocabulary can make up 1%, 50% or even 90% of a subject. If you are the slightest bit unsure of a word or term, stop and look it up. This is not a waste of time, but you can waste your time if you continue on past these terms without stopping and looking them up to clarify your understanding. I know I've said this before, but believe me, I haven't said it enough.

Each subject has its own vocabulary and is like a new language when you first come to it. If you look up the words and symbols as you go along, practice, use them and be patient, your fluency will come slowly, but it will come if you stick with it. Learning anything may seem difficult and complicated at first, but if you take it a step at a time, you can get it.

Words Within Words

Many times, while in the process of looking up one word, you will need to look up a second. This is a new word you are unsure of and it is part of the definition of the first word. At times, this can become rather involved, and you can find yourself looking up a whole string of words. This is one of the best possible and most fruitful exercises for your mind. As you do this, be sure to keep a list of the words you look up so you will not become confused or lost. Many students will find themselves looking up a string of 5 or 10 words to truly understand the original word. It is not uncommon to look up a great number of words at first while you begin to practice this habit of increasing your vocabulary, but it becomes easier and more fun as you continue.

There are many books with lists of vocabulary words to study, memorize and use. Feel free to use and study them. However, I feel increasing your reading to a wider range of materials will give you more meaningful and lasting training. In addition, it is more fun.

Guessing

Many times you can guess at the meaning of a word from the context of the sentence or paragraph. Often this will suffice for your immediate understanding of the word, but at some later time you should look it up. Otherwise, you may end up in the woods, because you thought you knew what it meant and did not stop to look it up and check. This can confuse and frustrate you in reading; also, it can cost you more time than looking up the word in the first place.

If you don't know the complete and correct meaning, you may substitute your own partial or incorrect understanding for what the author is saying. Following this, you may think that the author doesn't make sense or doesn't know what he is talking about when really you are the one with the problem. This can happen with simple words as well as complex ones, so you'll want to look them up as well. What is the definition of "by", "for", "a", "with", "to", "the", and so on? Go ahead, don't be embarrassed. Look them up and check yourself.

Some people never really learn to use a dictionary at all. It is not surprising that many times their understanding of the world around them is poorer than it could be. What they are reading or hearing is not necessarily what the author or speaker is saying.

People should at least be familiar with the instructions and directions at the front of their dictionaries. Some dictionaries will list words with the most commonly used meaning first while others will list the meanings in the chronological order of their evolution. This can affect what you think the dictionary says the word means. The dictionary is a true storehouse of information, but you need to learn how to use it correctly and effectively to benefit fully from it.

We use words to communicate with each other, and the dictionary is our common set of rules for what our words mean. Without using it, our communication is limited and uncertain. Over and over again, students make mistakes, get confused and do not understand what they are trying to read. This is where they may decide they are "stupid" or of low ability and quit. There is a solution: use the dictionary. I keep stressing this because no matter how fast or slow you go, you cannot read what you do not understand. If you do not understand, it is your responsibility.

At times you will need to consult special dictionaries in order to learn the definitions and usages of technical terms. These often have a particular meaning in the discipline you are studying, while they may mean something entirely different in general usage. Usually, it is fairly easy to spot this situation, and your librarian will be happy to help you find the necessary reference materials.

Along with using your dictionary, knowing prefixes, suffixes and roots is helpful, although you need not memorize them. The following are among the most commonly used:

Some common prefixes are:

Prefix	Meaning	Examples
ab	from	absent, abdicate
ad, ap, at	to	adjoin, apply, attire
be	by	beside, behind
con, com, col	with	conductor, commercial, collection
de	from	deduct, defrost
dis	apart, not	discolor, disappoint, disarm

Prefix	Meaning	Examples
en, em	in	entwine, entitle, embrace
ex	out	export, exhale
in, im	in, into	income, impose
in, im	not	impure, invalid
ob, of, op	against, away from	obstruct, offend, oppose
pre, pro	before, in front of	prepare, prenatal, propose, projectile, promote
post	behind	postpone
re	back	reply, repel
sub	under	subsonic, subject
super	over, above	superior, supervisor
trans	across	transpolar, transship
un	not	unhappy

Some of the more common suffixes are:

Suffix	Meaning	Examples
al	pertaining to	formal, musical
ble, able, ible	capable of being	forcible, available
ence, ance	state of	repentance, persistence
er, or, ist, ian	performer of	consumer, visitor, dentist, physician
ful	full of	careful, beautiful
ic	pertaining to	metric, artistic
ly, y	in the manner of	truly, stony
man	one who	cameraman
ment	result of, act of	argument, management
ous, ious, eous	like, full of	joyous, laborious, nauseous
ry, ty, ity	condition of,	finery, safety, purity
tion, sion	act of	temptation, decision

Here are some of the most used Latin roots.

Root	Meaning	Examples
fac, fact, fic	to make or do	facile, faction, fiction
fer	to bear, carry	transfer, ferry, infer
mis, mit	to send	submit, admission
mov, mot	to move	movie, motion
par	to get ready	prepare, repair
pos, pon	to place, put	pose, possible, opponent
port	to carry	portable, porthole
spect, spic	to look, see	inspection, conspicuous
sta, stat,	to stand	standby, stationary
tend, tens	to stretch	tendon, tension, extend
ven, vent	to come	venture, convention
vid, vis	to see	vision, provide

These lists are not comprehensive, but they do include many of the prefixes, suffixes and roots you will see most often in general reading. As with all words, there is more than a single meaning for most of these. If you only knew one meaning and assumed it was the correct one in every case, you would end up misunderstanding many words and messages. This is why you need to be sure you have the correct meaning and usage of each word as you read, and it is critical when you study.

The reader has the task of taking each word, each piece of the puzzle and reassembling it correctly in his mind. When there are many possible meanings, you must choose among them for the most appropriate. If you are correct, you will understand fully and read easily and quickly. If not, you will have difficulty, get confused and likely wonder what you are reading.

Codes

To a large extent, reading is working with codes. Each symbol stands for something. The author has encoded the information in words and you must decode it. Look these words up in your dictionary if you're not sure what I mean, because it's the key to our code.

Now do you see what I'm saying?

Your ease of understanding is your key. If the material makes sense and you can follow it well, then you probably are understanding it correctly. You are decoding it correctly and getting the message. This does not necessarily make what you are reading true, as we shall see later, but it does indicate that you are correctly understanding what the author is saying. The final test of your understanding is how well you can use what you have read.

Vocabulary is your key to accurate reading. You may have to look up the meanings and search for the correct definition, but when you do, you are going to be able to read and comprehend well and easily. Everything said here is generally applicable to all communication. It can help you communicate in listening, speaking and writing as well as reading.

Textbooks often include glossaries of specialized terms. Usually these are found in the back of the book. You should use them as frequently as you can.

Memorizing vocabulary is okay, but looking words up as you see or hear them is far more effective. Those you need you will retain, because in your daily life you will be using them, not losing them.

Chapter 25

How to Research an Area

Researching an area is our next topic of discussion.

Throughout this book I have refrained from going into details about reference works, the Dewey decimal system and how libraries are organized. What I have done is to encourage you to go into your library and get acquainted. There is a reason.

When you are interested, you will learn quickly if the materials are available. All the information, instructions and directions you need on where and how to find things are offered at your library. Librarians are trained, and usually eager to show you what is readily available and how to utilize it to its fullest. And most important, the actual materials are there when you want them for you to see, touch and use, not just to read about.

Cover All Sides

Nevertheless, there are a few suggestions I would like to give you about researching an area. Everyone wishes to do some form of research at one time or another, and there are a few mistakes that can be avoided. The most common error is to stop too soon, not covering enough information.

A good place to start any research is with encyclopedias. Then go to a periodical reference work such as the *Reader's Guide to Periodical Literature*. Keep a reference list of articles and books to read. Whenever something relevant is mentioned, be sure to add it to your list.

You should also work your way through the library's computer or card catalogues using the subject and author indexes. Then there are lists of books currently in print and reference works for various books and journals. Your librarian will help you here, but don't stop with just one or two references.

At some point in every student's life, he graduates from textbooks. Textbooks present information in an organized, non-controversial manner. Every issue generally appears to be firmly agreed upon and settled. Usually a student is shocked when the realization hits that everything in the world isn't like this. In fact, there is controversy, ongoing research, discovery and discussion in almost every subject and area of life. Knowledge, like life itself, is ever-changing and evolving.

In each subject, there exists a spectrum or range of viewpoints. There are respected experts from one side to the other with differing interpretations or views. It is important that you search out varied opinions and views and not just settle for the first one you meet. Only in this way can you come to an informed viewpoint of your own.

How do you do this? Take a stack of books, magazines and journals on a subject and preview them all. Isolate divergent opinions. Look at its history and evolution. Get a good idea of the whole field. Then work into the different views, and finally, master the facts on which the differing views are based.

Do internet searches, but don't believe the first thing you see or, necessarily, everything you read. Compare the information with other sources and references. Compare differing views with mainstream references before you make up your mind.

Defend and attack all the positions as you form your own conclusions. Do further research, look around you, check your own observations wherever possible, and most importantly, think for yourself and keep an open mind.

That does not mean to ignore or ignorantly attack the established opinions merely because they are established. Question them by all means and think for yourself, but realize, too, that a great deal of thought, research, discussion and argument have already been applied to these positions. Study them and form your own opinions.

Creativity and Knowledge

The world has advanced because of man's willingness to challenge, to search, to look anew, to think creatively and independently. In school, you usually are graded on how well you can do on exams compared to everyone else. Too often, this requires little more than memorization and recitation several times a semester. If this is the case, it is up to you to push yourself further into a field and discover its interesting aspects. They always exist; you can find them.

Sometimes it is hard to get through the numerous labels which are used to describe what is observed in any subject. But once you push past them, you will find experts debating whether they are truly correct, how to apply them to observations, how to measure or use information more accurately and effectively, and about what new work is being done and how it affects previous findings. This is where the excitement is. If it isn't being offered to you, you should push your way through to it.

Knowledge is everchanging and truly fascinating as a result. You may start a research project because it's assigned, but if you want, you can make it fun. Going that extra mile can make the difference between dull learning and enjoyable learning. It is up to you to decide how far to go in your learning and research, but don't stop too soon if you want to have fun.

Reading and Study

What we have covered on study is what I have found to be most effective for myself and my students. But while I want you to try to use these techniques, I do not want you to follow blindly or believe. I want you to apply this data on research to the field of study itself. Look, examine and decide for yourself the best study procedures for you.

There is a great wealth of information available on study and technical reading. If you intend to read much technical material or to study, you will find it well worth your while to look further into this area.

Laia Hanau in *The Study Game*, offers an outstanding, innovative presentation of her views on study and note-taking. She feels you should receive a serious communication, analyze and note it in a form she designates as Statement-Pie. You should look at and note what is being stated, how it is proven, what information is given to back it up and what are the examples used. This is the Statement-Pie or Statement-Proof, Information, Example. It is well worth reading.

There is also a classic work in the field. It is by the established authority, Mortimer J. Adler. His book, entitled *How to Read a Book*, is used in many schools and extensively discusses analytical and critical reading. It is strongly influenced by his experiences with the Great Books program, and you may find it interesting.

Another excellent book on study is *How to Study* by Ron W. Fry.

If you feel you need extra help from a tutor, you can look into the programs offered through your local schools and libraries. The schools in your area may offer study, reading improvement or speedreading programs, and you can inquire about them. They may also keep a list of recommended tutors; this is another possible resource. Perhaps the best source of information and help for you will be, once again, your local librarian. In almost all cases, your local library is an excellent source to consult.

The references I list in the bibliography can be a starting point for your own research. Look them up and make a list of other references to pursue as you read them. Try the techniques for yourself, and at some point, you will feel you know enough and can read and learn as you wish. This is when you know you have enough tools to do the job.

To help you do this faster, let's look at another tool, an advanced preview technique.

Chapter 26

An Advanced Preview Technique

You probably have noticed by now that in some materials it is difficult to keep your regulator up with your eyes. This usually happens in fairly easy or familiar material, in narrow columns or when previewing to get a general idea of what the material is about. To help you in these situations, here is a new regulating pattern.

It consists of moving your finger, pen or pencil down the page in a back and forth or "S" pattern. It is the same regulating motion you have been using except it is deepened to cover several lines at a time instead of just one line.

Your eyes still are moving from left to right, line by line most of the time. At times, though, you may want only the gist of what you are seeing. In this case, you naturally will tend to look at several lines at a time as you move from left to right.

At first, you should only be using this pattern to get a general idea of what you will be reading or have read previously. You should not expect, because it is unrealisic for most people, to be able to read word by word with full comprehension in this manner. This technique is for preview or review. When you need or wish to read with full comprehension, if you are like most people, you will need to read every word consciously or, at least, most of them.

When using this technique, you do not need to worry about what your eyes are doing. They will be consciously seeing key words and phrases as you get the gist of the material. If you get even more comprehension, that's excellent; but it's a bonus. I do not expect you to be able to read in this manner, but using it will help you to speed up as you preview and review.

Use the "S" pattern for preview, review and speed drills.

As you preview, if you come across a main idea or something else of particular importance and want to slow down to read it carefully, then do so. Simply change from this "S" regulating pattern to the normal underlining pattern. When you finish reading this key portion, switch back to the "S" pattern and your speed will pick up again.

Remember, the real key to Power Reading is slowing down and speeding up at will. You do not want to read everything at one rate, but you want to vary your rate so that you can get everything you need and want and still cover the maximum amount of material.

Chapter 27

3rd Week's Exercises

This week you may choose between two exercises, a new one for study or the one from last week. Do either daily. You should pick out some study, technical or non-fiction material this week and use the techniques we have covered for these types of material. If you already have been reading this type of material, then apply these techniques to it. If you usually don't read difficult material, pick a topic that interests you and research it for your own enjoyment. Try sports, ecology, economics, science or politics. If you are not sure what subject to pick, use the bibliography in the back of this book for study and reading improvement. If you are a student, you should definitely do this. Your librarian will be happy to help you.

Exercise One:

1. Go to your local library and pick up 7 non-fiction books in an area that interests you.
2. Pick one and preview it in no more than 5 minutes — covers, title page, table of contents, index, introduction, summary and conclusions. Dip in and out of it for the flavor.
3. Read it for 10 minutes, if you wish.
4. Review this material in 2 minutes.
5. Do this daily with a different book, each related to the same topic.
6. Complete each book if and when you wish. Use your technical reading or study method.
7. If you can't think of another topic, then use Study, Speedreading, Rapid Reading or Reading Improvement. Use the books listed in the bibliography and/or any others included in your local library.

Exercise Two:

1. Set aside at least 15 minutes to read.
2. Quickly look over what you can read in 10 minutes. Try to do this in 30 seconds and take no more than one minute.
3. Read for 10 minutes.
4. Cover this material again in 5 minutes. Be sure you cover it all in the allotted time. Remember, this is practice for speed.
5. Fill in your daily log.

Remember, we're already halfway there. Do your daily practice, and it will get easier from here on.

Supplemental Reading:

This week I suggest you read Huston Smith's classic book, *The World's Religions: Our Great Wisdom Traditions,* Harper Collins Publishers Inc., New York, 1991. It is one of the classic books on the world religions and humanity's spiritual traditions.

Log 3rd Week

15th Day:

    Today I read _____
                  (name of book or type of material)

    for _____
              (amount of time)

16th Day:

    Today I read _____

    for _____

17th Day:

Today I read _____

for _____

18th Day:

Today I read _____

for _____

19th Day:

Today I read _____

for _____

20th Day:

Today I read _____

for _____

21st Day:

Today I read _____

for _____

4th WEEK – LESSON IV

*Knowledge is of two kinds – we know a subject ourselves,
or we know where we can find information upon it.*
Samuel Johnson

Chapter 28

Fundamentals Again

Welcome back for the fourth time. I hope you have had another productive week. Here we are at the fourth and final lesson of this course. Actually, we have covered a great deal of material in the past three weeks, and as you read now, you should be using most of the fundamentals you have learned. Are you?

Are you looking ahead first at what you are going to read and finding out what it is about before you read it? Are you approaching the material based on this information and what you want and need? As you read, are you in control of your speed? Does it vary with your purposes, familiarity and the particular type of material? And certainly you are using a regulator on most everything you read, aren't you?

You know now that increased comprehension comes both from a correct understanding of the words and terms you see and an active multiple reading process. If you are a student, you should be using the study techniques given in the last lesson; and for your technical reading, you should be using a similar, individualized approach. In all cases, you know that your retention of the material depends on you actively using it.

As you have come through this course, you have used the techniques and not just read about them. You know from this experience that they can only be as effective as they are applied. This is even truer of the techniques we will cover this week.

163

This week, we are going to examine further the relationship between reading and the process of thinking. What does it actually mean to be an active reader? How do you do it? How does thought relate to reading? What should you be thinking about as you read? Are these separate processes, and if they are related, how do they relate? These are just some of the questions we will explore in this lesson.

They will lead us to our next topic, "How Do You Know If It's True?" This is the most important question to ask and answer for yourself as you read. We shall cover some simple principles that can help you to determine the answer for yourself.

Then we will see how to look at and cull through a large amount of material with new regulating techniques. Their use to help you preview, review and skim faster will be explained. These can also be the basis for advanced, high-speed reading if they are used and practiced for extended periods of time. Then, how to learn these skills will be the next subject. Included will be the necessary drills and procedures to use if you are interested in working on "high-speed" reading techniques.

As you can see, we have a lot to cover in this lesson as well, so let's begin.

Chapter 29

Reading and Thought

The fact that reading affects thought, thought affects reading and both affect each other at the same time is an important factor in Power Reading. How are they interrelated? Do you or can you control this relationship? If so, how?

We'll begin our examination of these questions by looking at the vase below.

Vase

Do you like it? Take another look at it. Do you still feel the same way about it, or do you see something else there? Perhaps you see two identical faces in profile, looking at each other? Do you see them now? Of course, once they have been pointed out, you cannot miss them.

This illustrates the point that, to a large extent, what you look for, you will see. This holds true in reading as well as in much of life. By telling you what to look for, by putting the thought in your mind, I helped influence what you perceived. This happens innumerable times every day, and it comes from many sources.

Prejudice is one example of this in life. Assume that you were brought up to expect certain things of people who belong to a particular sex, race, religion or age category. Then one day on your job, you find out you have to work with such a person. At first, you expect that what you have thought to be true will be demonstrated. Yet, after several months of working together with this person, you find out that your previous conceptions were actually misconceptions. This person is another human being just as you are. Certainly there are differences and similarities between you, but they are not outside the range of what you can experience and bridge over with most people.

Change

Before you had this experience for yourself, you thought a certain way based on the information you had. What you saw was labeled by the vocabulary already in your mind. This new experience changed your vocabulary, and consequently, what you expected and looked for around you would have changed. The data and experiences you have, which you think with, are different now. Your actions in life will differ as a result. More than most people realize, what you look for and expect in life will occur. This is why positive thinking programs succeed.

Your mind serves as a mental map and dictionary. It contains all of your previous experiences, thoughts and ideas. Your past, stored in your memory, contains the data you use to weigh alternative actions, to predict their consequences and to decide which actions to take. Based on what you have done in the past, you decide what is the best thing to do in the future. This process is not always a conscious one, and it is similar to how the mind functions when you read.

Earlier we covered how perception worked as it related to reading. Subconsciously, the mind picks out the next point on which to fixate before you consciously see it. Based on what you have read, it decides what you should read next and interprets it accordingly. Below your level of consciousness, many things are happening while you read. Everything that comes in is related not only to what you are reading now, but also to everything that you have read and experienced. What you are reading is mentally condensed and abstracted so that while you cannot remember it verbatim, you can recall its summarization and many of the details and facts.

What you are reading is being cross-referenced, catalogued and compared to similar data in your memory. In fact, it is stored in relation to everything you know. Of course, you're not conscious of this at the time; you're only aware of seeing and comprehending the words as they appear.

At the same time, what you are reading prepares you for the next word, sentence or paragraph. You anticipate and even may read something into what you are reading. It could be something that the author did not put there, or you could rearrange the emphasis to change what is important. This happens a great deal with readers.

Effectiveness

An effective reader is aware of this, and because of his many tools for correct and rapid understanding, it is not a problem. The effective reader will actively question, probe and examine while reading. What is the author saying? Why is he saying it? Does it make sense? Uncertain words are not allowed to pass with only a guess at their meaning. Therefore, comprehension is smooth. Where it is not, the effective reader goes back to discover why. This is the basis of Power Reading.

The effective reader has time to reread the material when it's necessary, and this multiple reading process ensures greater understanding.

The Power Reader reads within the context of the whole. This comes from previewing. Reading, like driving, is easier and clearer if you know what road you're on, where you're going and how the individual part you're traveling over relates to those preceding and following it. By looking at the map first, you can choose the easiest, most direct route and arrange time for peaceful sightseeing. If you simply start out, you may not make it in time and your trip can become rather hectic.

Power

This doesn't mean you have to plan everything in advance. Quite the contrary: when you know you can accomplish what you need to, you can relax more when you wish. This is power, the ability to go at the speed you desire and to go where you wish and see what you like.

This is not all. Besides these tools, a Power Reader has another important advantage. We have seen how the mind takes in data, correlates it and stores it away for future use. When a new situation comes up, the similar information from the past is drawn upon to help predict consequences of various actions and select the best one. This is true whether a person is deciding and acting as an individual or in some other capacity such as the head of a family, group or business. The goals, the position, the information or the constraints may differ, but the decision-making process is the same. It is based on the available information.

The Power Reader, the effective reader, has a tremendous advantage over others in that she has access to a much wider range of data. It is true that reading is not the same as actual experience in life, but there is a limit as to how much activity can be packed into a single lifetime. The boundaries of experience can be increased enormously by reading, and only in this way can the boundary of time be crossed.

You can learn not only what others think and do around the world today, but also what they thought and did in earlier times. Even in the midst of this changing world, some things remain the same. Certain thoughts and problems have confronted mankind for centuries, and the valuable work done by our ancestors should not be ignored or thrown away. Reading is the key to this information.

Evaluation

There is another important factor here. Your experience in life is seen from your own viewpoint. Often you can expand your horizons and understanding of what has happened and is happening by finding out what has happened to others in similar circumstances. This way, the boundaries of your thought processes and the limits of your mind can be expanded. And this can help you to make better decisions.

There are no quick, simple rules for correctly relating what you read to your own life. Learning to do this comes from reading and trying out what you learn. You will begin to note and weigh the evidence of experts and others in any given field and experiment for yourself. As you do this, many of the older ideas and misconceptions that you had picked up will be discarded. At the same time, many new ideas and understandings will be gained.

This process of exchanging older, narrower patterns of thought for newer, broader ones is the basis of man's social as well as individual evolution. At one time, our ancestors would fight, and perhaps kill, anyone of a different tribe; new ideas were suspect. It has taken thousands of years for these mental barriers to fall and for us to begin to realize that our continued survival depends on our cooperating and working together. A glance at the daily news makes it apparent that we have not yet completed this process. But make no mistake, we have made advances and we are continuing to make more.

There are other factors concerning reading, thought and experience that are significant. One is the relative importance, or weight, given to reading versus experience. Normally, what you read is less real to you than what you experience personally. It has less weight in your memory and often less in making decisions.

169

The importance of what you read and the confidence you have in this information are directly related to your experiences in life. For example, you read about next season's fashions and then you see them. You read about money in school and then you use it in everyday life. If you neglect to read the sign with the speed limit and get a ticket, then you learn. You talk about ideas with your friends, and you find out what they get from their reading and what they think. You learn to evaluate what is important in your reading.

There are many things you read about that you cannot see immediately in your daily life. However, they too affect you. Among these are politics, economics, international relations and most scientific advances. The only experience you might have with many of these subjects would come through reading. In order to understand them fully, you may well have to read more. And as you read, particularly in controversial areas, you will discover a great range of opinions and viewpoints. Whom should you believe? How do you know what's true?

Chapter 30

How Do You Know What's True?

Here's where all your reading skills come into play.

Philosophers have spent thousands of years discussing this question. They have come up with countless theories and spent untold hours arguing various positions. Unfortunately, they are no closer now to a final answer than they were when the discussion began.

So how can we do this when the wise men have yet to succeed? How can you tell whether what you're reading is true?

In an absolute sense, you can't. As history moves along, every idea, viewpoint and piece of information has been superseded by new and more advanced theories. These new ideas are accepted because they explain data which are contrary to or outside the scope of earlier explanations. Thus Copernicus' theory supplanted Ptolemy's, and we came to see the Earth as circling the sun instead of the other way around.

Nevertheless, there are clues to help us evaluate the truth. One key to this knowledge is comparison. The comparison of one idea, fact or system to another is an integral part of man's thought and development. Observations are made and compared to one another. Man observes something at one time, again at another time and then compares the two. For example, man has observed the stars for thousands of years. The observations are collected and noted. Similarities and differences are noted. Theories relate the observations, explain the comparisons, similarities and differences, and to the extent they are correct, accurately predict the future. Further observations or experiments are then made to check the theories.

When mankind no longer looks, observes and compares, knowledge stops. This is true in all cases. It is true for a group, nation or race as well as an individual.

On the other hand, the eternal flow and change of knowledge may confuse and overwhelm an individual's understanding. What other clues can help solve this mystery and dispel the confusion? There are several.

First of all, does the internal comparison of one part to another within the theory show consistency? Is it consistent throughout the whole, or are there inconsistencies and contradictions? Are the terms clearly stated? Are they used in the same way from one part to another? Do the internal parts make sense by themselves, are they based on facts or do they depend on some outside authority or source for their importance? If so, on what does the external source depend?

This brings us to the next factor, external consistency. How do the ideas, viewpoints, interpretations and facts presented compare with others in the field? There is a great deal of difference in viewpoint and interpretation among the experts in most fields. How do they compare? Which explanation is simpler and requires the fewest assumptions? On what do the experts agree and on what do they disagree? And finally, what do you see? What makes sense to you? This is the crux of the issue.

Your Own Viewpoint

You must be the final judge for yourself. This is the basis of our modern civilization and our survival.

You can study a single person, school or viewpoint; you can memorize and learn it cold, but you won't have data with which to compare it. This is like being a student of one of the three ancient blind scholars who studied the elephant. One felt the trunk, another the tail and the third the leg. Each one described the elephant differently, and needless to say, they couldn't agree on what an elephant looked like. If you studied under only one of them, you would have only his idea of what an elephant was. If you studied under all three, however, and compared the similarities and differences, then you could truly begin to form your own more complete viewpoint.

That indeed is the purpose of an education in a free society. The purpose is not to be a puppet who can mouth the correct words for an exam or on command, but a free thinking, independent person capable of individual judgment. This can come only from looking at a wide range of data and thinking on your own.

Willingness to Change

Your opinion won't be expert at first, but don't be afraid to have one. On the other hand, as you get more data and experience, be willing to change your views. Allow them to expand and grow. Look for new facts and views to challenge and extend your own.

Another aspect of external consistency is the set of facts themselves. What are the facts of the author's position? Are they stated correctly? Are they complete? Many times there is not enough data to come to a final conclusion. Is there another explanation, and if so, what could it be? How does this compare with your own experience in life? What are the author's sources? Are they reliable? Is the author reliable? What are his qualifications? What do others have to say?

In every field there is a hierarchy of recognized authority and opinion, but this doesn't make it always correct. Once, one of the world's leading scientists proved flight was impossible for a craft heavier than air. The next year the world saw the first flight of Orville and Wilbur Wright. This was not the first time experts were wrong, nor the last. No matter what experts or established authorities say, you are entitled to your own opinion. However, the fact that you have a right to an opinion doesn't make it correct. Even though most people believed the world was flat throughout much of history, the world retained its shape. Once new facts were brought back by Columbus, opinions began to change.

The Questions to Ask

The most important questions to ask concerning what you read are:

1. Is it internally consistent?
2. Is it externally consistent with the facts?
3. Are you really checking out the facts through research and/or your own experience?

No simple reading and memorization will tell you if what you are reading is true. You will have to compare the source to other sources, viewpoints and experiences. The fact that something holds true in one, two or even several cases does not mean that it holds true in most cases or in all cases. Thus, individual successes need to be compared to a wide range of experience. This always is true, whether it is a medical cure or a business solution.

You must not look just at the white or black situations, but also at all the shades of gray in between. There are always exceptions to every rule and examples at the extreme. You always want to look at the large picture before you settle on a single position.

You must look at what is actually on the page. What does it say? Is it said clearly and consistently? Does it make sense? You must look beyond the page. What experience is it based upon? How valid is this view? You also must look at your own experience, both in life and from other reading. Is it consistent with what you know? How does it compare and relate to other sources of information? And finally, how well does it work? This is the final and most important question. This is the one that can best tell you if what you are reading is true.

In order to answer these questions, you will need to look at a great deal of information. You will need to see and compare many things. The next techniques will help you do this.

Chapter 31

Speedy Speedreading —

High-Speed Techniques

In an earlier chapter, we saw how some experts argued that it was impossible to read faster than around 900 wpm. Yet, there are some people who can read faster and comprehend excellently.

Throughout history, there have been people who could do this. John Stuart Mill was one. Samuel Johnson was another. So was Sidney Web, the English economist who co-authored with his wife, Beatrice, more than 50 books. Teddy Roosevelt was well known for his phenomenal reading capabilities, and another United States president, John F. Kennedy, was also an exceptionally fast reader.

How?

How is it possible for some people to be able to do this? In any activity or endeavor the level of skill involved varies from individual to individual. Reading is no different, and all readers have their own natural ability. Here is an explanation of how advanced readers use theirs.

The mind can take in 4 or 5 items each short-term cycle. These are usually letters or words, but they can also be ideas. The idea can represent the meaning for several words or a phrase. Since you have the natural ability to see an inch of a line with a single fixation, you can take in this much information. This is the horizontal dimension of a fixation.

It also has a vertical dimension. It is possible to see sections of several lines with a single fixation. And in some cases, especially in easy or familiar material, the mind can integrate this information to obtain the correct meaning. While this happens, you would be conscious only of seeing key words and phrases.

This happens when the information you already have allows you to fill in the gaps and piece together what you are seeing. Let's look at a simple example using letters in a sentence.

C_n y__ r__d t__s?

Perhaps you can understand, or decode, the above line from your understanding of what you have been reading. At high speeds you might be piecing together key words or ideas in a similar manner. If you couldn't understand them from the information you've seen, given the mental context created by what you have been reading, you would go back over the information again looking for more pieces to fit together.

Can y_u r__d th_s?

Probably, you have it now. If not, the answer to "Can you read this?" was no and is now yes.

This same process occurs with ideas at high speeds. You piece them together rather than individual words.

You may not be able to do this easily. In most cases, it is either a natural talent or one that must be developed by many hours of practice. Only experiment will tell you to which category you belong.

You Can Benefit

There is no need to worry. Even if you are not a natural, "speedy" speedreader, you can benefit from these techniques and drills. This is because these techniques can be used to preview and review, as well as read, at very high speeds. They are excellent for looking over a great deal of information for comparison, searching for specific answers or reviewing previously studied material.

The emphasis here will be on introducing these techniques to you and showing you how to work and practice more effectively with them. The degree of competence you will achieve with them depends on how much time and effort you wish to expend.

Preview and Review

These techniques are presented primarily as previewing techniques. I recommend you use them as such. They are best used to cover a lot of material to find out generally what it says, to see how the arguments are laid out and to compare differing views. You may want to locate main ideas quickly and then slow up to read them thoroughly. This is how to cover a great deal of material that is not worth reading slowly. This is also how to understand more when you preview. Learning how and when to do this will take practice, but it is a skill well worth acquiring.

The techniques presented earlier in this book required that you use them, but usually when you tried them in your daily reading, they were easy to apply. Results began immediately, and some progress was apparent without too much difficulty. These advanced techniques will take more work and persistence. It may take several weeks to several months of hard daily practice before you can achieve meaningful results at high speeds, 700 – 1,500 wpm.

Many people do not wish to put in the effort. This is an individual decision. It does not mean that they have failed in some way; it means that they have decided that they have no need to take in information at such high speeds. These people feel that they have achieved enough when they are reading 10 percent faster, half again faster, or twice as fast as previously. This is sufficient to meet their needs in daily life. If they wish to read even faster at some later time, the instructions and drills are contained in this book.

I am not trying to discourage you, but this course is not a race. You are learning and working to achieve your own goals. Only you know when you can read fast enough and well enough to fulfill your own needs and desires in life.

Try This Week

Before you make a final decision, however, I want you to try these techniques and drills over this next week. Get some experience with them; they will help you. Then you will have a good idea of how far you want to go and how much work it will take you. You will achieve some degree of competence with them, and you never will forget the basics. They will come back to you easily if you wish or need to pursue this skill in the future. Thus, this week will help you with your present and future progress. If you ever need or want to do research or cover a large amount of material, you will know the most effective techniques for doing so.

Many readers do not desire or find it practical to become "speedy" speedreaders. This was stated earlier. Comprehension and appreciation of details usually fall out at higher speed. In order to read faster, the mind must necessarily condense the information. Words and phrases often become impressions. Practice and rereading to check your comprehension are necessary to build confidence in your accuracy at these speeds.

This is easier to do when you are just trying to get the information than when you are living the story. You usually want information as quickly as possible. Living the story is something you may want to last.

Not all courses make this distinction. Many push you to read faster continuously on everything you read. We have discussed the machines that many programs use to do this. Some use techniques similar to those used in this book, such as use of the hand for regulating patterns.

All courses push you to read faster, then allow you to slow down. The rate you slow to will be slightly higher than the one at which you started. Then you repeat this process over and over.

Some courses try to teach you to push on everything. This isn't correct. It isn't natural. There are times when you want to sprint, but there are also times when you want to jog, and there are many times when you want to walk. These high-speed techniques are for sprinting.

How is it then that many courses guarantee to triple your reading efficiency? This term is a calculated figure. It is arrived at by multiplying your reading speed by your percentage score on a reading test. We have already discussed some of the problems associated with reading tests. Some courses use their own tests, and not all of them are standardized for accuracy. Occasionally, tests are fairly easy. In all cases, high speeds will outweigh lower comprehension scores.

This is a major reason why many students are not entirely happy with their results from speedreading courses. It stems from trying to use high-speed techniques on all types of materials and trying to read everything at superfast rates. You can achieve similar results from the following techniques and drills, but I suggest you don't.

I suggest you use them for practice and as preview or review techniques. This way they will gradually work into your kit of reading tools. This method will give you more permanent results because these techniques perform best as special tools used to supplement, rather than replace, normal reading.

Now let's look at these new techniques. The first ones are new regulating patterns. As you try them, you may or may not get any comprehension at this point. If you do, once again consider it a bonus. If not, you can practice with them until you do get some. Then you can use them for previewing, practicing and some reading as you wish.

Turning the Pages

You will be going over the material much faster than you have in the past and you will need to be able to turn the pages more quickly. This is done by holding the book and turning the pages with the same hand. The other hand is used as your regulator as it was in the past. If you regulate with your right hand, then you will hold the book and turn pages with your left hand as shown below. If you haven't been doing this since Lesson I, now is the time to start.

Turning Pages

Try turning the pages in this manner for a few minutes. If the book is new or won't stay open easily, gently bend it open and flatten the pages. Be careful not to break open the binding or the pages can fall out. This is why it is important for you to use a bookmark and not leave a book lying on its face. It tends to break down the binding and ruin the book, a needless waste.

New Regulating Patterns

You should try these regulating patterns on earlier parts of this book or pick up another book. It is best to practice on something you have already read or some fairly easy material.

The first is the "S" pattern. If you haven't used it this past week, then try it now. Spend at least two or three minutes using it.

The "S" Pattern

The next is a "Z" pattern. Remember, you are just trying to get the gist of the material, generally trying to follow along with the author's ideas if you get any comprehension at all. Do not worry about details or facts; just try to follow the main idea. Your finger stays on the page as you move horizontally from left to right, slashes down to the left across several lines and repeats this process down the page. Try it for a few minutes.

The "Z" Pattern

This next one is the "slashing Z" pattern. It is similar to the last one except you lift your finger from the page as you move it horizontally from right to left. The names of these patterns aren't too important. They simply describe the motion of the finger or regulator on the page. Try this one for a few minutes.

The "Slashing Z" Pattern

Here is the spiral regulating pattern. Your finger stays on the page. Try it.

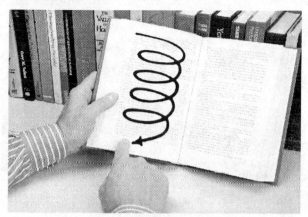

The "Spiral" Pattern

The next one is the looping pattern. Try it for a couple of minutes.

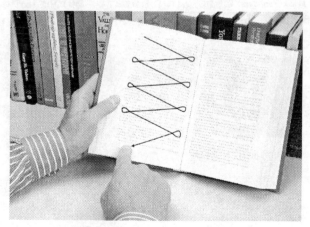

The "Looping" Pattern

This next regulating pattern is wiggling down the page with your whole hand. There is no mystery or mysticism involved. It simply gives your eyes a little more time with the material. Try it for a few minutes.

The "Wiggling" Pattern

In this next one, your finger or whole hand moves straight down the page. Now, try this one for a few minutes.

Coming Down the Middle of the Page #1

Coming Down the Middle of the Page #2

You can do the same using a 3x5 inch card.

Using a 3x5 Inch Card

The next is one of my favorites. I use it and the "S" most for high-speed reading and previewing. You hold the book with your left hand. Your right hand is the regulator and you use it coming down the right margin. On the left page, you use your index finger on the margin.

185

Down the Margin #1

On the right hand page, you grasp the page between index finger and thumb and come down the outside margin. This makes it easy to turn when you reach the bottom of the page and to start again on the next left hand page. Try this one for a few minutes.

Down the Margin #2

Down the Margin #3

Now look back through these high-speed regulating patterns. Pick out the two that felt the most comfortable and natural. Then go through this book for a few minutes more using only these two hand motions. Do it as quickly as you can, and remember, this is practice.

Did you notice how you can spot the main ideas? When you preview, often you will locate the main idea and want to slow down to read it carefully. When you complete reading the main idea, continue previewing the material by switching back to the faster regulating pattern.

The more you read, the more you will be able to differentiate between important information and filler material. Filler material deserves little more than a quick glance, whereas important information warrants a careful reading.

It is a skill you should work on as you do the following drills during the next week.

Chapter 32

High-Speed Drills

In doing these drills, you can use any of the regulating patterns, from underlining each line to coming down the margin. As you go faster, you gradually will progress to the more advanced patterns.

You also need to write the summaries called for in the drills. This forces your mind to focus and comprehend so that you will be able to write something. Even if it's not too much, write something down on your summary sheet. You can use one of the note-taking methods given in the note-taking chapter if you wish. You can write an essay summary. You can also write a short summary in which phrases and key words are all that are necessary. You do not have to write full sentences. The emphasis here is on practicing reading, not spending a lot of time on writing unless you wish to do so.

To work on reading at these high speeds, you will need to do two or three different drills daily, each at different times. Or you can repeat the same drill two or three times daily with intervals in between each practice session. You should begin to see gains in one or two weeks, but these are likely to fade unless you keep up your practice. Usually, it takes one to three months of daily practice for any permanent high speedreading results to develop. Here are the drills.

5-3-1 Drill

1. Read for 5 minutes. Mark ending spot.
2. Write summary — 1 minute.
3. Practice over the same material in 3 minutes.
4. Add to summary — 1 minute.
5. Practice over the same material in 1 minute.
6. Add to summary — ½ minute.

7. Repeat steps 1 – 6 in new material, same book.
8. Read for 5 minutes in new material, same book and compute wpm.

Add on Drill # 1

1. Read for 5 minutes. Mark ending spot.
2. Summarize — 1 minute.
3. Add on ¼ more pages of new material, same book.
4. Practice over material plus additional ¼ in 5 minutes.
5. Add on to summary — 1 minute.
6. Repeat steps 3, 4 and 5.
7. Once again, repeat steps 3, 4 and 5.
8. Read for 5 minutes in new material, same book and compute wpm.

Add on Drill # 2

1. Read for 5 minutes. Mark ending spot.
2. Summarize — 1 minute.
3. Add on ½ more pages of new material, same book.
4. Practice over material plus additional ½ in 5 minutes.
5. Add on to summary — 1 minute.
6. Repeat steps 3, 4 and 5.
7. Once again, repeat steps 3, 4 and 5.
8. Read for 5 minutes in new material and compute wpm.

Extension Drill # 1

1. Read for 3 minutes. Mark ending spot and count number of pages.
2. Multiply number of pages times 6.
3. Mark off this number of pages in new material, same book.
4. Preview this material — 3 minutes — start summary.
5. Practice over this amount of material in 10 minutes — add to summary.
6. Practice over this amount of material in 3 minutes — add to summary.

7. Read for 5 minutes in new material and compute wpm.

Extension Drill # 2

1. Read for 10 minutes. Mark ending spot and count number of pages.
2. Multiply number of pages times 6.
3. Mark off this number of pages in new material, same book.
4. Preview this material — 5 minutes — start summary.
5. Practice over this amount of material in 20 minutes — add to summary.
6. Practice over this amount of material in 10 minutes — add to summary.
7. Read for 10 minutes in new material and compute wpm.

When doing these drills, particularly in the beginning, you should choose fairly simple material that you have read before or material you are familiar with and can understand easily. This will make it easier for you to comprehend and write the summaries. Speed is what you will be drilling and working on most. Push yourself to get over all the material in the allotted time when that is what is required.

No Substitute for Reading

There is no limit to how long you can use and benefit from these drills. No matter how fast you read, they can help you. As you progress, you can begin to use more difficult material. Do this in a gradual manner; work your way up slowly to more and more difficult material. But don't expect a quick practice to substitute for careful reading or study, because it won't. When you read, be sure to get what you need and want from the material.

All of these drills are designed to work from your present individual reading level. Many courses use metronomes, electronic beepers or other machines to emit sounds at short intervals. You are supposed to read a line or a page every time you hear the sound. In some courses, an instructor will periodically tap on a desk or call out signals to accomplish the same function. You can try this with a friend, but it forces you to go at an arbitrary pace that is unrelated to your basic reading speed. Also, there is no room for variance because of the importance of a particular line or paragraph. In a class, it forces everyone to go at the same pace regardless of individual rates. This is why we don't use this type of drill.

Throughout this book, I have given you my opinions on other methods, programs and techniques and what I have found from my own research and teaching experience. My system shares parts with many others, but it is unique in emphasis and execution. Naturally, I prefer my own system, but I want you to compare and form your own opinions. Every program can help the person who wants to learn. With what you have learned from this one, you should be able to learn from the others more quickly. Further reading and study in this area can only increase your skill, so if you haven't already gone to the library to study other methods of reading improvement, you should definitely go and do so this week.

Try this book for your high-speed drills. Try the drills on all types of materials. Experiment and see how fast you can read. Push yourself. If you lose the path of comprehension, slow up a little until you get enough to write your summaries. But don't slack off. Really try to extend yourself and increase your range. Full comprehension can be obtained with a later rereading; be sure to do this when it's needed and wanted.

At this point in the course, you should be reading between half again faster and twice as fast. Around 70 percent of the students fall within this range while the rest are divided evenly above and below this band. Look back at the goal you picked in Lesson I and see how you are doing. How are you doing in relation to Lesson III, the halfway point? How well are you doing now? If you are off your target, then buckle down for a tough week. Do plenty of drills for your best bet to achieve your goal. You can do it. I have confidence in you.

Chapter 33

4th Week's Exercises

This week you have a choice among all the high-speed drills. Do at least one daily.

Remember, if you have not yet visited the library, this week is the time to do so. You should look up the references and other works listed in the bibliography.

Use a variety of materials, push yourself and have fun.

Supplemental Reading

Consilience: The Unity of Knowledge by Edward O. Wilson, Vintage Books, New York, 1998. Paperback. This book discusses humanity's relationship to the universe from a scientific perspective and our responsibility to each other, our planet and all its inhabitants.

Log 4th Week

22nd Day:

Today I read_____
(name of book or type of material)

for_____
(amount of time)

23rd Day:

Today I read_____

for_____

24th Day:

Today I read_____

for_____

25th Day:

Today I read_____

for_____

26th Day:

Today I read_____

for_____

27th Day:

Today I read_____

for_____

28th Day:

Today I read_____

for_____

30th DAY

Originally, "common sense" meant "understanding or knowledge based on the evidence of the senses," as opposed to mere suppositions, superstitions, or fancies, which could not stand up to a practical or empirical test.

Lindgreen / Byrne

Chapter 34

Final Exam

Hello, again. Well, here we are. For 30 days I've been teaching and you've been learning. You've been reading in this way, using the techniques, regulating yourself, speeding up and slowing down as desired, breaking down old habits and establishing new ones. You already know for yourself what you have put into this course and what you have achieved from it. You probably have already established a pretty good subjective opinion. Now let's do another 10-minute reading like the initial one and see how much you've improved according to objective numbers.

Take the book you used in the initial reading and the mid-course exams. Quickly reread those portions and look at your summaries of this material.

Now read for 10 minutes in new material.

All right, go ahead and begin reading.

Very good. Summarize as fully as possible what you've just read in the last 10 minutes. Do this on the Final Reading Summary.

FINAL 10-MINUTE READING

Final Reading Summary

Date:_____

Book Title:_____

Page began reading:_____

Page ended reading:_____

Summary:_____

_____

_____

_____

_____

_____

Now Let's Compute Your Present Speed.

Multiply the average number of words per page (Answer 4 from Lesson I) by the number of pages you read this time and divide by 10.

_____ words per page (Answer 4 in Lesson I, page 9)

X_____ pages read in final 10-minute reading

=_____ total number of words read in 10 minutes

Now divide by 10:

$$\frac{\text{(total number of words read)}}{10} = \underline{\hspace{4cm}} \text{(your final speed in wpm)}$$

Now write down your initial speed and that date and your final speed and today's date.

$\underline{\hspace{3cm}}$ wpm initial speed on $\underline{\hspace{3cm}}$
(date)

$\underline{\hspace{3cm}}$ wpm final speed on $\underline{\hspace{3cm}}$
(date)

How do they compare?

You can see your percentage increase by doing the following:

Divide the difference in these rates by your initial speed and multiply by 100.

See the example:

EXAMPLE:
Initial wpm = 264
Final wpm = 528
528 - 264 = 264 (difference)

$$\frac{264 \text{ (difference)}}{264 \text{ (initial wpm)}} \times 100 = \underline{} 100 \underline{} \% \text{ increase.}$$

Now calculate your results:

$$\frac{\text{(difference)}}{\text{(initial wpm)}} \times 100 = \underline{\hspace{3cm}} \% \text{ increase.}$$

This is how much faster you are reading now than when you began this course four weeks ago.

Now let's answer the same comprehension questions.

1. Did you feel you understood what the author said?
   Yes _____ No_____
2. Do you feel you got the main ideas?
   Yes _____No_____
3. Do you feel you got the basic facts?
   Yes _____No_____

Check yourself and find out how accurately you did read the material.

Quickly Reread the 10-Minute Selection to Check Your Comprehension

Now look at your summary again, and then answer the following questions.

A. Did you understand it as well as you thought earlier?
   Yes _____ No_____
B. Did you understand the main idea/ideas correctly?
   Yes _____ No_____
C. Did you get the basic facts?
   Yes _____ No_____
D. Did you get enough the first time to satisfy you as you look back now?
   Yes _____ No_____
E. Do you feel you can more effectively read and comprehend this material than when you started this course?
   Yes _____ No_____

Why?

_____

_____

_____

_____

_____

_____

_____

_____

Well, your answer to this last question brings us to the conclusion of this course.

Chapter 35

Conclusion: Power is Knowledge Plus Common Sense

Power usually refers to the ability to do things and the rate at which they can be done. Obviously, the more you can do within a specific time span, the more you are able to accomplish, and the more choices there are available to you. You are more powerful if you can do more, and you have increased your freedom.

Data consists of facts and observations made or noted at some time and place. Because of some interest of yours, you focus attention on this data, and it informs you about the object of your interest. The data is passive; it simply sits there. You are the active, interested portion of this process. You focus your attention and play it over the data. In return, you are enlightened or informed by it. It becomes useful information when it is defined by and used in the context of what interests you.

When this information is understood in the light of your experience, it can be said to be evaluated. It is evaluated not only by what you know intellectually, but also by what you know from the totality of your experience, or common sense.

Common sense tells you that few things are black or white, but that most things are various shades of gray. It tells you that absolute rules can be memorized, but experience is crucial to a successful selection of what rules to apply in what situations and to what extent. Common sense tells you that you can swallow things whole and uncritically, but that the best approach is to use a grain of salt for your own individual seasoning.

All the data in the universe is of no use to you without focusing your attention to light it up and allowing it to inform you. Information that is unevaluated by your own experience may be memorized, but cannot be really known.

Fortunately, we live in a time, a society and a situation in which this decision is up to you. You can decide how much power you will have. You will decide how much you can know and use as the base of your actions. You can decide how fast or how slowly you wish to take in and use new information or old.

If you now consider reading to be akin to driving in that you can look quickly at the road or a map to see where you are going, if you understand that the more times you travel the route, the better you will know it, if you realize that you can start or stop and get on or off the road as you consciously wish, then you understand what I have been trying to teach you.

Power Reading is being able to read fast or slow, once or many times, completely or partially, for study or pleasure, or somewhere in between, but always as you choose to achieve the goals you have selected. If you know how to do this, you know how to Power Read. If you do this, you are a Power Reader.

What you do with this power is up to you, just as how you read now is your decision.

You no longer need to use a regulator. I usually don't, and I certainly don't expect you to either. You have probably noticed by now that you still read about twice as fast even when you don't use a regulator. This will vary depending on the type of material and your familiarity with it, but it usually averages around double your original rate.

When you read for your own enjoyment, you should let your rate be secondary to your pleasure. I find that the more I enjoy a book, the more I slow down when reading it. I want to make it last longer. Savoring a good book is one of my prime enjoyments and I hope one of yours.

Reading for speed alone is a waste of time; understanding is what is important.

What should you read? Well, what interests you? Libraries, bookstores and the Internet are packed with data. You can turn this into useful information and knowledge. You can use it to create the quality of life you wish to have or to continue.

What we know plus our common sense is the basis of humanity's success. Once all the members of our race, the human race, were cavemen. Then, most of our time was used in a savage struggle for survival. Slowly we have come together, cooperated and gained knowledge. With this knowledge we have created our civilization as well as its difficulties; we can solve the latter as we have done in the past.

Knowledge and common sense are the keys for unlocking the solutions. Everything is possible and ahead of us. We are just beginning to discover how the universe is put together and what place we can create for ourselves in it. There are no limits except those placed by our immediately available data and our previously made agreements.

Every day new discoveries are being made, and you can help to make them. You do have power in the world and can affect it with the power of your reading.

I hope you use your reading power to help yourself personally, to help your family and to help your fellow man. If you do, and enough of us do, the changes will be amazing.

Thank you for taking this course. I hope you have enjoyed it as much as I have, and I look forward to exchanging ideas with you once again in the future.

BIBLIOGRAPHY
Books:

Adams, Royce W., *Increasing Reading Speed,* Macmillan, New York, 1969.

Adler, Mortimer J., and Van Doren, Charles, *How To Read A Book,* Simon & Schuster, New York, 1972.

Armstrong, William H., *Study Is Hard Work,* Harper & Row, New York, 1967.

Baldridge, Kenneth P., *Reading Speed & Strategy For The Business and Professional Man,* Prentice Hall, Upper Saddle River, NJ, 1966.

Barr, R., Kamil, M.L., Mosenthal, P.B., Pearson, P.D., editors, *Handbook of Reading Research,* Vol II, Lawrence Erlbaum Associates, Publishers, Hillsdale, NJ, 1996.

Bloom, Harold, *How to Read and Why,* Touchstone Books-Simon & Schuster, New York, 2001.

Carter, Rita, *Mapping the Mind,* University of California Press, Berkeley, CA, 1999.

Chall, Jeanne S., Ph.D., *Learning To Read - The Great Debate,* McGraw Hill, New York, 1967.

Crick, Francis, *The Astonishing Hypothesis: The Scientific Search for the Soul,* Simon & Schuster, New York, 1994.

Deese, James and Morgan, Clifford T., *How To Study,* 2nd Edition, McGraw-Hill Book Company, New York, 1969.

Donahue, P.L., Voelkl, K.E., Campbell, J.R., Mazzeo, J., *The NAEP 1998 Reading Report Card for the Nation and the States,* U.S. Department of Education. Office of Educational Research and Improvement. National Center for Education Statistics. NCES 1999 - 500, Washington, D.C., 1999.

Dowling, John E., *Creating Mind: How the Brain Works,* W.W. Norton & Co., New York, 1998.

Eccles, John C., *The Understanding Of The Brain,* McGraw-Hill Book Company, New York, 1977.

Fader, Daniel, *The New Hooked On Books*, 10th Anniversary Edition, Berkley Publishing Corp., New York, 1976.

Flesch, Rudolf, *Why Johnny Can't Read and What You Can Do About It,* Harper & Row, New York, 1955.

Fry, Ronald W., *How to Study,* 5th Edition, Career Press, Franklin Lake, NJ, 2000.

Greene, Brian, *The Elegant Universe: Superstrings, Hidden Dimensions and the Quest for the Ultimate Theory*, Vintage Books, New York, 2000.

Hanau, Laia, *The Study Game,* Harper & Row, New York, 1974.

Harris, Albert J., and Sipay, Edward R., *How To Increase Reading Ability,* 8th Edition, Longman, Inc., New York, 1985.

Harris, Margaret and Hatano, Giyoo, editors, *Learning to Read and Write*, Cambridge University Press, Cambridge, UK, 1999.

Johnson, Ben E., *Learn To Rapid Read,* Howard W. Sons & Company Inc., New York, 1973.

Keene, Ellin Oliver and Zimmerman, Susan, *Mosaic of Thought: Teaching Comprehension in a Reader's Workshop,* Heinemann Publishing, Portsmouth, NH, 1997.

Kohl, Herbert, *Reading, How To,* Open University Press, Stony Stratford, UK, 1988.

Landes, David S., *The Wealth and Poverty of Nations: Why Some Are So Rich and Some So Poor,* W.W. Norton & Company, Inc., New York, 1999.

Lorayne, Harry and Lucas, Jerry, *The Memory Book,* Ballantine Books, New York, 1975.

Lorayne, Harry, *Super Memory — Super Student,* Little, Brown and Company, New York, 1990.

Manguel, Alberto, *A History of Reading,* Penguin Books, New York, 1996.

Mathews, Mitford M., *Teaching to Read: Historically Considered,* University of Chicago Press, Chicago, 1966.

Moidel, Steve, *Speed Reading for Business,* Barron's, Hauppauge, NY, 1998.

Morehouse, Laurence E., Ph.D., and Gross, Leonard, *Maximum Performance,* Simon and Schuster, New York, 1977.

Orwell, George, *Animal Farm,* Signet Classic, New York, 1996.

Pitkin, Walter B., *The Art of Rapid Reading,* Grosset & Dunlap, New York, 1929.

Reading Laboratories, *Cut Your Reading Time In Half,* New York, 1957.

Reading-Study Center School of Education, *Speed Reading; Practices & Procedures,* Volume X, March 1962, University of Delaware Press, Newark, DE, 1962.

Sagan, Carl, *Billions and Billions: Thoughts on Life and Death at the Brink of the Millenium*, Random House, New York, 1997.

Smith, Frank, *Understanding Reading: A Psycholinguistic Analysis of Reading and Learning to Read, 5th Ed.*, Lawrence Erlbaum Associates, Inc., Hillsdale, NJ, 1994.

Smith, Huston, *The World's Religions: Our Great Wisdom Traditions*, Harper Collins Publishers, Inc., New York, 1991.

Smith, Nila B., Ph.D., *Speed Reading Made Easy*, Reissue Ed., Warner Books, New York, 1994.

Sweet, A.P., and Anderson, J. I., editors, *Reading Research Into the Year 2000*, Lawrence Erlbaum Associates, Publishers, Hillsdale, NJ, 1993.

Waldman, John, *Rapid Reading Made Simple*, Doubleday, New York, 1958.

Weinland, James D., *How To Improve Your Memory*, Harper & Row, New York, 1976.

Whimbey, Arthur and Linda, *Intelligence Can Be Taught*, E.P. Dutton & Co., Inc., New York, 1975.

Wilson, Edward O., *Consilience: The Unity of Knowledge*, Vintage Books, New York, 1998.

Articles:

Berger, Allen, "Questions Asked About Speedreading", *Clearing House*, January, 1970.

Borhan, Babak, et.al., "Movement of Retinal Along the Visual Transduction Path", *Science*, Vol. 288, pp. 2209-2212, 23 June 2000.

Brown, J. I., "You Can Read Faster", *Readers Digest,* May, 1970.

Dembo, Myron H. and Wilson, Donald A., "A Performance Contract in Speed Reading", *Journal of Reading,* May, 1973.

Graf, Richard G., "Speed Reading: Remember The Tortoise", *Psychology Today,* September, 1973.

"Look's Twenty Day Course In Quick Reading", *Look Magazine,* February, 1970.

Miller, L. L., "Speed Reading In The Seventies", *Education Digest,* September, 1973.

Paulesu, et. al., *Dyslexia: Cultural Diversity and Biological Unity,* Science, Vol. 291, pp. 2165-2167, 16 March 2001.

Smith, Brenda G., "Speed Reading Scores in Perspective", *Journal of Reading,* November, 1975.

Spache, George D., "Is This A Breakthrough In Reading?", *The Reading Teacher,* January, 1962.

Stahl, S.A., Duffy-Hester, A.M., Dougherty-Stahl, K.A., "Everything you wanted to know about phonics (but were afraid to ask)", *Reading Research Quarterly,* Jul/Aug/Sep, 1998.

"Sure You Can Learn To Read Faster: Is A Speed Reading Course Worth The Money?", *Changing Times,* November, 1973.

Witty, Paul A., "Rate Of Reading — A Crucial Issue", *Journal of Reading,* November, 1969.

Standardized Testing:

Birrell, James, and Ross, Sandra K., "Standardized Testing and Portfolio Assessment: Rethinking the Debate", *Journal of the College Reading Association,* Summer, 1996.

California Achievement Tests, Reading California Test Bureau, McGraw-Hill.

Houts, Paul L., editor, *The Myth Of Measurability,* Hart Publishing Company, Inc., New York, 1977.

Iowa Silent Reading Tests, Harcourt Brace Jovanovich.

Mavrogenes, Nancy A., et. al., "Concise Guide To Standardized Secondary and College Reading Tests", *Journal of Reading,* October, 1974.

Nelson Denny Reading Test, Houghton-Mifflin.

Stanford Achievement Tests: "Advanced Paragraph Meaning; High School Reading", Harcourt Brace Jovanovich.

INDEX

Achievement, 16 – 19

Blind Spot, 74 – 75

Brain, 76 – 78

"Breaking In" a book, 39

Common Sense, 34, 70, 98, 201 – 203

Comprehension,

    building confidence, 49, 59 – 60

    definition, 45 – 49, 148

    difficulties, 98

    improvement, 45 – 50, 55 – 60, 111

    improvement drill, 50

    measurement, 3 – 5, 10 – 12

    mental dictionary, 82 – 84

    no substitute, 69 – 70

    special terms, 98 – 99

    test averages, 12

    understanding, 69 – 70

    versus drilling, 71, 112, 114,

Computer,

    files - naming, organization and retrieval, 124

    screen reading, 93

Concentration,

    attention, 28

    improvement, 49 – 50

    study, 134 – 137

    warm up, 28

Consilience, 64

Correspondence, 13

    email, 108

    mail, 107

Cosmology and the Structure of the Universe
    "The Elegant Universe", 64
Deprogramming Yourself, 58 – 59
Dictionary, 46, 82 – 83, 98, 123, 132, 148 – 149
Discomfort with Regulator, 62
Encyclopedias, 153
Experience, 97, 170, 201
Eye, 73 – 79
Fixations, 76, 84 – 87, 175
Glossaries, 152
Habits, see Reading, habits
Holding the Book, 40, 51 – 52
Information Explosion, ix, xiii, 22
Internet,
    file naming and retrieval, 124
    information validity, 154
    searches , 154
Kennedy, John F., 28, 175
Legal Materials, see Technical Materials
Libraries, 2, 4, 63, 92, 105, 124, 153, 156, 203
Looking at the Whole,
    3 Q's, 29 – 32
    definition, 24, 27 – 32
    drills, 31 – 32, 112 – 113
    preview, 24, 27, 134
    study, 134, 140
    technical reading, 124 – 126
    usage, 24, 27 – 29
    warm up, 28
Mathematics, 63, 138

Memory,

long-term, 127 – 129, 137 – 140

short-term, 78, 83, 175 – 176

Page Turning, see Turning Pages

Perception, 73 – 80

Perception Span, 43, 84, 86, 92

Plays, 109

Pleasure, 109

Poetry, 109 – 110

Power Reading,

exams, 6 – 12, 117 – 122, 195 – 199

family participation, xv

goals, 19

how it differs from other courses, x, xv, 89 – 93, 191 –192

how long it takes, xiv – xvi, 63, 178

how much improvement you can expect, xiv – xvi, 13 – 19

how to do the course, xiv – xvi

plateaus, 60

pleasure material, 33, 109 – 110, 202

practice defined, xv, 111 – 114

practice required, ix, 59 – 60, 111 – 114, 177 – 180

results, xiv – xvi, 17 – 18, 177 – 178

scheduling the lessons, xiv – xvi

test material selection, 5 – 6

what it is, 13, 21 – 25, 158, 163 – 164, 167 – 169, 202 – 203

why you should learn it, 13 – 19

Practice Defined, 111 – 114

Preview,

an advanced technique, 157 – 158

computer and online material, 106

definition, 24, 27 – 32, 55

Preview (continued),
  looking at the whole, 24, 27 – 32
Problem Solving, 41 – 43, 59 – 65, 102
"Readers Guide to Periodical Literature", 153
Reading,
  accuracy, 10 – 12, 46 – 49
  and thought, 165 – 170
  changing habits, 38, 41 – 43, 55 – 60, 88 – 93, 111 – 114
  comfort, 41, 52 – 53, 69 – 70
  comprehension, 3 – 5, 45 – 50, 55 – 56, 59, 69 – 70, 81 – 84, 111 – 113
  computer screen reading, 93
  correspondence, 107
  definitions, 1, 148
  dislike for, 63
  email, 108
  enjoyment, 33 – 35, 109 – 110, 202 – 203
  habits, 3, 23, 25, 27, 32, 34, 37 – 39, 41 – 43, 49, 55 – 59
  illiteracy, 21 – 22
  independence of mind, 33 – 35, 106 – 107, 154 – 156, 172 – 174
  Internet, 124, 154
  learning how to, 81 – 84
  opinions on, 23, 170 – 174
  phonics, 81
  regressions, 57, 86 – 87
  single rate, 23
  slowly, 81 – 88
  speed, 1 – 3, 12, 17 – 19, 56 – 57, 67 – 69, 79 – 80, 177 – 179, 202 – 203
  tests, 2 – 5, 209
  to waste time, 34

Reading (continued),
     too fast, 21, 112 – 114
     tools, 24 – 25
     versus drilling, 71, 111 – 114
Regressions, 57, 86 – 87
Regulator,
     comfort, 41
     computer mouse cursor, 93
     definition, 37 – 38
     discomfort from, 62
     embarrassment from, 38 – 39
     finger, 37, 41
     high-speed, 158, 181 – 187
     problems with, 60
     shortened regulating, 67 – 68
     usage, 55 – 62, 92, 111 – 114, 202
     using pen or pencil, 51 – 53
     why one is used, 42 – 43
"Religions, the World's", 64, 206
Religious Reading, 110
Rereading, 57, 59, 92, 141
Results, xii – xvi, 17 – 18, 177 – 178
Scanning, 79
Skimming, 79, 101, 164
Socrates, 1
Speedreading,
     advertising, xiv, 179
     comprehension, 17 – 18, 178 – 180
     Evelyn Wood Reading Dynamics, xiii
     high-speed techniques and drills, 175 – 194
     how it works, 175 – 177

Speedreading (continued),

    learning how to do it, 175 – 194

    machines, 42 – 43, 89 – 92, 191

    no magic, 42

    "reading efficiency" score, 179

    results, xiv – xvi, 13 – 19, 58 – 60, 121 – 122, 178 – 180, 198 – 203

    "speedy", 175 – 194

    tools, 58 – 60, 191 – 192

    upper limit, 79 – 80

Study, 127 – 142

    five steps, 140 – 141

    lectures, 131 – 132

    length of sessions, 127 – 128

    logical units, 134

    memory systems, 140

    motivation, 129 – 131

    note-taking, 132 – 137, 138 – 142

    other books on, 156

    preparation, 132

    review, 125, 137 – 141

    study reading, 134 – 136

    test taking, 141 – 142

    the 3 keys, 133 – 134

    time management, 132

    use it or lose it, 138 – 139

Subconscious, 58 – 59, 76 – 78, 87 – 88

Subvocalization, 57, 87 – 88

Technical Materials, 95 – 108, 123 – 125, 127 – 156

Textbooks ,

    glossaries, 152

Textbooks (continued),
    logical unit studying, 134
    time management, 132
Troubleshooting, 41 – 43, 59 – 65, 102
Truth, 171 – 174, 201 – 203
Turning pages, 39 – 40, 52, 180 – 181, 186
Use It or Lose It, 138 – 139
Varying Speed, 24, 37 – 43, 56, 111 – 114
    regulator use, 37 – 38
Vocabulary, 83, 97 – 98, 123, 147 – 152
Work Materials, see Technical Materials
WPM,
    averages, 12
    computation, 8 – 10
    definition, 8
    upper limit, 79
Your Approach,
    computer and online material, 106
    correspondence, 107 – 108
    definition, 24, 33 – 35
    for different materials, 95 – 99
    magazines, 101 – 107
    multiple reading, 35, 124, 133
    newspapers, 101 – 106
    pleasure reading, 109 – 110
    study, 127 – 142
    technical, 123 – 125

Notes

Notes

Read what students, parents, educators and business professionals have to say about Power Reading:

My comprehension is greatly improved. This increase in my comprehension is as important to me as the increase in my reading speed. Definitely recommend it.   J. Morabe, Executive

I am surprised at how much faster I can read. I realize it is possible to cover more material without losing comprehension.
     M. Clement, R.N.

Power Reading has been really helpful in dealing with manuals, etc., and with getting through needed materials.
     A. Lashbrook, Supervisor

I have always hated to read and now I am able to get into it more. I feel my comprehension has improved. The Power Reading textbook was very good. I recommend this course to others.
     R. Harden, Food Service Supervisor

Power Reading has taught me how to process the "wheat from the chaff" in the mounds of paperwork sent daily. This gives me the opportunity to spend more time on those items essential or preferable.   G. Jones, Executive

With the ability to cover more ground, together with the taught previewing practices and faster reading, I feel I can cover the material faster. I can also cover it more than once and thus learn it even better when I need to.   R.S. Cannell, Associate Planner

This course was much simpler than I had expected, yet covered all the essentials. I'm much more comfortable with reading; I'm flowing more smoothly and picking up more information while reading faster.   B. Copeland, Production Mgr.

My reading speed and comprehension have just improved so much — and already I am driving people crazy because I just want to read everything. I purchased your course, because at age 45, I have recently changed my career and gone back to college to study IT (Information Technology). M. Fox, Student

*Based on the outstanding results achieved with my son, Michael, in the **Power Reading** course, I felt I should sit down and write a thank you. We started Mike on your course because he was considered by his teacher to be a "problem reader." Within two weeks he was already beginning to see a difference that shocked even him. The results achieved were surprisingly quick and the effort quite minimal. Your methods are far superior to any others I have seen and cannot help but work with even the minimal amount of effort.*
Before, Mike did not like to read. Now Mike is busy reading with a tremendous amount of enthusiasm for which I am eternally grateful to you. I really believe this was the best possible thing I could have done to further my child's education and keep him on the track to higher learning.
He was far behind his class; now he's way ahead. I think that's something to be proud of! Again, my deep appreciation.
  J. Carlson, Parent

I enjoyed the class and I certainly increased my speed. I recommend it. S.K. Emiti, Student Nurse

It improved my comprehension as well as my speed. This was my goal. I. Dinkin, Domestic Engineer

*Six years ago, I took a speedreading course, and afterwards, promptly fell back to my old rate. Amazingly, with **Power Reading**. I doubled my reading rate and am still improving. I wish I'd taken this course six years ago.* L. Gomes, Consultant

***Power Reading** has helped speed up my reading and saved me time. My job demands a lot of reading for screening items for routing to my staff and other important materials. I used to read so slowly, I was always behind, now I'm keeping up.*
  J. Edlund – Executive Director, Girl Scouts

*It definitely is terrific. It gave me the ability to read much more material, together with increased comprehension. **Power Reading** left me with the ability to get the information much faster than before. This way I have more time for pleasure reading. The course was more than I had hoped for.* B. Holm, Secretary

This course gave me a lot of help. It helped me with both my speed and comprehension, as well as my concentration. I found the course enjoyable. J. Barrara, Student

This course was really helpful. I have improved my comprehension and I read faster. L. Lopez, Student

*The benefits of **Power Reading** were not simply limited to advances in reading speed, but also included increases in comprehension. In a large agency such as this one, increases in reading speed and comprehension of management staff will greatly facilitate business operations.* P. J. Tighe, Staff Development Supervisor

My concentration is greater... presented in a positive manner. It is a very good course. I have been able to apply the techniques in my daily work and at home. B. Baker, Executive

Completely satisfied... simple techniques and they work. Prepared me to take my state board exams and allows me to power skim occupational journals and materials. N. Wilson, Architect

*I took the course to learn techniques and improve my speed. I got both without a loss of comprehension. **Power Reading** has helped me with reviewing large amounts of material in my job and with my pleasure reading. I like the compact nature of the course, use of the book, and techniques and materials.* J. Willin, Executive

For one who has to read as much as I do, this course saves hours a day! P. Cooper, Executive